FREE
AND
HOLY
WHERE YOU ARE

The Daily Life of a Catholic

MSGR. DENNIS M. REGAN

ISBN 978-1-64569-683-4 (paperback)
ISBN 978-1-64569-684-1 (digital)

Christian Faith Publishing, Inc.
832 Park Avenue
Meadville, PA 16335
www.christianfaithpublishing.com

Printed in the United States of America

WELCOME!

I hope this is the beginning of a journey together which will take an open and **honest** look at how followers of Jesus can enjoy more fully the freedom which should invigorate our daily lives. I am a practicing and joyful Roman Catholic priest with an earned doctorate in theology and many years of service in parishes, theological education, pastoral formation, and spiritual counseling. Together we will look at some significant current and at times controversial issues, situating them in light of the refreshing freedom God wants for each of us. A grace for which I have always been thankful is one that unexpectedly surged in my heart on the day after I was ordained as a priest—*freedom* to witness to the *importance* of every person I hoped to serve by conveying God's *unconditional love* for each of us.

For many Catholics, including the religious culture in which I was raised, there was excessive emphasis on *saving your soul by keeping the rules taught by the Church*. Although not all the rules were easy to keep, it was a clear and focused message easy to preach and teach. Fortunately, since we have always lived in God's love, people's generosity often produced holiness and sanctity. But *keeping rules* for most people did not promote experiencing the joy and adventure of *freedom!* Hence for many committed religious people, a missing ingredient was *enthusiasm*. The Spirit seemed to use the Second Vatican Council (early 1960s) to uncover intriguing challenges, inviting each of us to a greater maturity and deeper spirituality. We were no longer *along for the ride* but must become a vibrant and living community of disciples of Jesus—a *Pilgrim Church* peopled by *co-creators with God of a redeemed but unfinished world*.

Why did I choose to title these reflections FREE AND HOLY WHERE YOU ARE: *The Daily Life of a Catholic?* Because our everyday lives as Catholics is truly God's invitation always to be free (self-directed as a follower of Jesus and as a member of the community of faith which is his body). Since Jesus is always *walking with each of us every moment of our lives* (*Do you believe this?*), the call to be free happens *where we are*: everyday life, work, family, friends, hopes, fears, dreams, disappointments, opinions, decisions, failures, successes, aging, growth—the stuff of life. So let us go forward reflecting on some of the things which make up our lives. But please let us read and consider them with *freedom* as our filter. No matter the specific topic, these examples all embody aspects of the *freedom* which is our gift. Experience through each how daily life calls upon our personal freedom to interact in a creative and exciting way. This is the challenge and the adventure.

We are living on earth at a singularly wonderful time. My final offering at the end of this book is "Emerging Creation" which briefly begins with the astrophysical science that I have never seen in a theological treatment. Our planet, after billions of years, became at last hospitable not only for the incarnation of Jesus, but human beings had developed as capable of participating in an exciting mission— that each of us could respond to God's love and presence by accepting that we are *co-creators of a redeemed but unfinished world.*

Dennis M. Regan

IMMERSION IN GOD

I'm sure we have all seen fish gliding through water—perhaps at home in our own fishbowl or in a public aquarium. It can be calming and almost mesmerizing at times. We can see that the fish are immersed in the water, completely covered, but it's even more than that because their bodies are mostly water and water travels in and out through their gills. Every part of them is touched by water, inside as well as out.

I have heard no better image to express how we, as human beings, are *immersed* in God. God surrounds us and penetrates our being internally, as well. The great mystic, Meister Eckhart, observed that everything flows from God, yet remains in God. "God in all and all in God." Our being made in God's image and likeness is complemented by a deep and inescapable *presence*—whether or not one believes in God's existence. It's just what a human being is. God doesn't simply give us life, call us by name, and then go off somewhere and leave us alone. Always respecting us as unique persons and our personal freedom, God's *delight is to be among the children of men.* So why would God ever leave them?

My favorite scriptural sentiment enshrined in our liturgy is prayed as part of Preface VI of the Sundays in Ordinary Time (cf. also Acts 17:28), "For in you we live and move and have our being." What we are trying to understand and then live every moment is fully expressed in those words. In God we live (every second of our lives), and move (every thought and action), and have our being (existence always flowing into us). This is not something simply to read and then move on. We cannot pay too much attention to this most profound and basic reality. The implications should change our lives—bringing meaning, hope, direction, peace, and freedom.

Are there ways to put this into practice so we don't forget? I'm sure there are many, but let me share something that helps me and many others I know. We believe that God's love and presence means God is constantly aware of the thoughts, emotions and desires, and actions of each of us at every moment. Make this real personally by frequently reminding ourselves that "God sees with me through *my eyes*; God hears with me through *my ears.*" When we are upset with someone, blessing someone, praying for something, frustrated, fearful, hopeful, rejoicing over something, frightened—and whatever else is in our conscious mind—God is already with us, sees and hears with us, and knows. We don't have to tell God about it, just a quick thought between the two of us accomplishes everything that matters. No one understands us more completely, is more *on our side*, wants even better for us than we ourselves do, and always loves us no matter what. Trust God.

WHY GAY?

Of all the major areas of Catholic teaching, it seems to me that *sexuality* needs the most attention. That may be for many, if not countless, reasons. In these reflections, we will consider a number of questions, clarifications, opportunities, critiques, alternatives, concerns, etc. to keep going a discussion on how best to let God's marvelous yet challenging gift of sexuality enhance our freedom. We begin with a commonly misunderstood question: *Why gay?*

For our purposes today, let's submit that there are basically two *sexual orientations* possible for a human being—heterosexual (opposite sex attraction) or homosexual (same-sex attraction). Those sharing the latter often accept the appellation: *gay.* We will use this term to refer both to men and to women who have a same-sex orientation. Not simply to be politically correct nor to imply a preferential judgment, let's use another simple term to refer to those who are heterosexual—*straight.* Though there could be questions and distinctions with what has already been said, our purpose here is to consider only: *what causes one's sexual orientation, whether toward the same or the opposite sex.*

To be fully a part of this endeavor, you must be willing to do any background research—if you want to explore or contest the sources of what I am presenting as *accepted fact* (my relying on those who are highly regarded in whatever field is treated: theology, scripture, science, psychology, etc.) This can easily be searched in Google. Very few issues in life are definitively settled, but I will seriously attempt not to over-or understate the sources or conclusions I will share with you. Please remember always that I am not trying to *sell* you anything! It is a further illumination of *truth* that we seek together, not a validation of *my* opinion (or for that matter, *your* opinion either!). Are we open enough and up to the challenge?

To the question at hand. Over the centuries many people have assumed being gay was a personal choice or preference and, therefore, could be changed. That is, God made and willed that everyone be straight but some chose to be gay and we must help or demand that they, too, become straight. (This is not some philosophical point. Human beings have been bullied, burned, or murdered for this.)

Over the last few decades, responsible scientific studies have shown that sexual orientation for anyone is determined in the womb, before birth, and before free choice is possible. Lady Gaga's song "Born This Way" is surprisingly accurate. Gays deserve no condemnation; straights deserve no credit. No individual *chose* her/his orientation.

So what about the 5 to 8 percent of any human population who are gay? A minority, yes. Misunderstood by much of our society, yes. Should they follow straight rules, date, and marry the opposite sex? No (though fear of prejudice has led many to this tragic and self-denying conclusion).

Some *homework* for each of us: imagine your beloved, popular, and terrific son or daughter is gay. The hateful and destructive prejudice of so many in their school, church, business, or society is ready to brand and exclude them from *normal* life. Suicide has looked good and has been chosen by many. God must be so *proud of us* for upholding God's *plan*. Don't you know some friend or relative who is gay? I do and have in my ministry and sat with many more wonderful gay people. They are our children, too, our relatives, our fellow believers, shouldering a burden over which they had no choice and made worse by our complicity in an ignorant and threatened society.

THE NEW NORMAL

In these days of considerable change on so many levels of life we've probably heard the phrase *the new normal*. I'm not so sure that the *old* normal was as great as we remember, but it's obvious that fairly recent events and circumstances are driving a number of people crazy! Let's look at a few—job uncertainty or unemployment, middle class income relatively stagnant for more than two decades, 401(k) s reducing savings for many, poverty still present even in our society, government and politicians seeming not to be up to the challenges, scandals in the church, unforeseen or denied climate changes worldwide. Because our purpose here is to develop attitudes which increase our personal freedom, it might be useful to consider some of the effects *generally*, and then *individually*.

Life for all of us is greatly influenced by the world which lies just outside our door. We can feel overwhelmed by so many changes on so many levels. Some people have been tempted to stop paying attention to the news, which I don't think is the answer. Hope is a virtue which was always necessary as part of the *old* normal of daily living and is even more demanded by the *new* normal which we really cannot avoid. We must realize the strengths that will still see us through—our own abilities and the support of family and friends, solid institutional structures which have survived even greater challenges over the years, the continuous presence of God for whom human evil (and strength) are no surprise.

Add to that environment the personal aspects of our lives. Perhaps we, too, are facing job insecurity or inadequate income. Maybe our parents are becoming more dependent on us, or grown children can't find meaningful work, or an unexpected or chronic illness can't be ignored. We've forgotten that *worry* accomplishes no good at all. It only wastes our time and saps our energy, distracting us from hope, courage, and action. Really, all *problems* ultimately come from within. The factors we've been observing are really *challenges*—but it's our attitude toward them which lets them become *problems*—weighing us down, paralyzing us. This is neither semantics nor smarmy word tricks. We must see them always as *challenges* which then can activate our creativity, hope, and spirit of cooperation.

Let's take just one example of what for many has become *the new normal.* One's grown child can't find work and he/she asks to move back home. The *empty nest* is put on hold! They and we never expected this, and it changes so much—for the young person as well as the parents. We might take them back, but it diminishes our freedom and theirs if we welcome them back as our *child!* There should be honest and ongoing discussion with her about respecting schedules, helping out regularly, and contributing financially to some degree. He will have to make sacrifices in taking seriously his responsibilities and realizing your home is not a bachelor pad (and no girlfriend staying overnight!). Everyone's space must be respected. This can be a great opportunity for all involved to grow in freedom and maturity, if no one lets a challenge become a problem.

Perhaps there should be one more beatitude added to the list Jesus gave us: Blessed is the person who can increase their freedom by seeing good possibilities in unexpected change!

OUR PILGRIM LITURGY

One of the terms popularized at the time of Vatican II—well over fifty years ago—was the *Pilgrim Church*. Born of humility, it acknowledged that the Roman Catholic Church didn't think it *knew everything*—just enough. A fitting image would be that of a *pilgrim* seeking a path and direction in unfamiliar lands—subject to detours, backtracking, and even choosing new routes toward one's destination.

[Just an aside (an important one though): do you think you know where this is going? Have you tuned out or speeded up because you don't agree or you've heard all the arguments against the position you favor? I thought we were both looking for truth and increasing our freedom. Could it be that you already have all the truth you need?]

Moving right along, as they say, let's take another image appropriate for the followers of Jesus—a *family*. His Church is a family. At this point, I want to be true to my own integrity and admit there are at least twenty-five (a hundred?) things/issues about this family that I can't stand. But that's for another day. Just as with one's natural family, you put up with the grief because of the good. I found Jesus Christ (or Jesus found me) through the Church—in his sacramental touch, the Word and word which are alive, people who believe and love and serve where we can know what good must be done, even when we don't do it. But whatever some authority's arrogance, ignorance, or their *we know best* of the moment—or even sinfulness or criminality or *cover-ups*—I will not let it push me away from all that incredible good. Do we distrust all police because there are some *bad cops?* Only Jesus is divine; all the rest of us are human. Take time to see the *full truth*.

Pastors say that for every ten parishioners there are at least five different opinions. Could even the latest attempt at liturgy be improved? No doubt—from whatever stance we take. Meanwhile, could we put everything else aside and just pray—with Christ and one another? Let's hope so. There's still a lot to pray for, pilgrim.

CONSCIENCE

There is among Catholics another area subject to a great deal of misunderstanding. That confusion truly limits the personal freedom that God wants us to become more aware of and enjoy. We could phrase it: "How am I expected to apply the Church's moral teachings to my life?" The summary word for that area is: *conscience.* Depending on how we have had it explained to us, some regard it as a negative: an imposition, limitation, maybe even a curse. But it's a core part of the human nature God designed—and God gives only blessings.

"Should we have meat or fish for dinner?" That requires a *decision*—a simple and every day one.

"My husband and I are convinced this is not the right time for another child, so we're thinking of using contraception." That requires a decision.

In wartime, one can't be at the same time a soldier to defend one's country and a conscientious objector to war based in a deep respect for all human life. Again, a decision—a choice, a commitment. Psychologists tell us we are *made who we are* by our decisions—*important* decisions can both express our deepest self and reinforce/refine that self. *Conscience is that unique power everyone has to decide here and now what one can and must do out of what ought to be done.*

Where do I discover *what ought to be done* in this situation? We are not born with nor should we individually create for ourselves the *raw material*—the values, truths, and wisdom—which should be the bases of our decisions. Rather than limiting our freedom, the best of human experience and the wisdom of lived history cannot possibly be replicated alone by any single one of us. All credible sources—education, family, society, secular and religious knowledge—all these and our own *common sense* and intuition must come into play.

Catholics believe that the *Teaching Church* (Bishops in union with the Pope and one another) is charged with the service of overseeing with the experience of the faithful, fidelity to the gospel, and the wisdom of the lived tradition of the Church—the followers of Jesus. This includes both doctrinal and moral teachings. As history readily shows, there has been, over the centuries, considerable development and growth in both areas.

In our time, decreasing respect for authority on the part of many has often interfered with the *speaking* and the *listening* which are essential to a necessary dialog serving truth. Any *decision in conscience* requires knowledge, not of a simple statement of a law or rule but of the values at its root. The person deciding/choosing must understand and evaluate the relevant factors or parts of what is at stake. She or he must be open throughout the deliberations to input from any credible source because at the time the decision must be made, it is made *alone with God whose voice echoes in his depths.* This is a deeply individual, personal, and sacred moment. It is *I* who must decide—a transcending moment of freedom; it is *my* decision—an awesome responsibility.

But what about the *confusion* and *misunderstandings* alluded to above? Some people think their freedom means "I can do whatever I want" with no meaningful input from anywhere else (egotistical, isolationist, childish?). Some reject any wisdom from the religious/faith area (limited, prejudicial, defensive?). Some reject their own responsibility to decide and want someone else (parent, spouse, priest) to decide for them (immature, manipulative, fearful?).

All that was said above about conscience and the right/responsibility of each person *always* to make his/her own informed decision regarding an action is a traditional teaching of the Catholic Church. For those with the responsibility of *teaching* in the Church, it may be tempting not to remind people that the decision how to act is ultimately theirs. Conscience must be regarded neither by the teaching authority nor the faithful as some *loophole* through which might slip someone who wants to escape a moral obligation. The teachings and moral values must be thoroughly and engagingly explained by those whose service it is to do so, but then each fellow member of Christ's body—the Church—must be trusted and supported *when they have decided in conscience that they are now doing what they can and must do out of what ought to be done.* There can be no sin here. She or he is doing the best of which they are capable here and now—and God does not demand the impossible.

As a type of *postscript,* may I reprint for you two authoritative citations. The first is from the great saint and theologian, Thomas Aquinas. The second is promulgated by the Pope and bishops in the documents of the Second Vatican Council:

"Every judgment of conscience, be it right or wrong, be it about things evil in themselves or morally indifferent, is obligatory, in such a way that anyone who acts against his conscience always sins" (St. Thomas Aquinas, *Quaestiones quodlibetales,* 3, q. 12, a.2).

"Deep within his conscience man discovers a law which he has not laid upon himself but which he must obey. Its voice, ever calling him to love and to do what is good and to avoid evil, tells him inwardly and at the right moment: do this, shun that. For man has in his heart a law inscribed by God. His dignity lies in observing this law and by it he will be judged. His conscience is man's most secret core, and his sanctuary. There he is alone with God whose voice echos in his depths. By conscience in a wonderful way, that law is made known which is fulfilled in the love of God and of one's neighbor" (*Gaudium et Spes,* no.16).

GOD, REAL AND NEAR

Karl Rahner, a brilliant and deeply spiritual German theologian influential in recently past decades, is noted for saying that "the Christian of the future would have to be a mystic."

Since this term *mystic* is so often misunderstood—especially as preoccupation with *New Age* writings and practices have spread—I was delighted to find in *Commonweal* (a respected Catholic periodical since 1924) a most valuable article titled "Nearer to God: Demystifying Mysticism" by Lawrence S. Cunningham, a teacher of theology at Notre Dame University (October 7, 2011). Let me make an attempt to share some helpful points for those who might not have access to the entire article (as some of our readers are in developing nations). My own appreciation of Rahner and his prescience leads me to take very seriously his warning above about the Christian of the future having to be a mystic. (Most of what follows are Cunningham's valuable citations but are not in *quotes*.)

What Rahner meant was that the traditional cultural support for religious observance was in a state of rapid erosion so that if a person didn't have a deep personal experience of the reality of God's love, there was little left to hold him or her to a conventional practice of the faith. Rahner believed that *God's self-communication* was at the heart of human experience. His critical point was that the experience of grace—that is, *the sense of God's presence*—was not something reserved for spiritual virtuosos but open to all.

When the great *mystic* St. John of the Cross wrote about mystical theology, he was writing from within a tradition in which his writing was not a technical or theoretical discourse but out of an experience of the triune God's incomprehensible love. John did not think of this experience as having anything to do with the extraor-

16

dinary experiences now commonly associated with the *mystic* locutions, raptures, etc. The foundational insight is that one must pass from the world of sin and disorder so as to see in a new way. Finally, in order to be open to a deeper experience of God's love.

All the mystics in the Christian tradition assumed that the person of prayer who sought a deep intimacy with God would participate in the ordinary means of holiness in the Church—regular prayer, participation in the sacraments, a sensible approach to asceticism, and the works of charity. Meister Eckhart said that if a person were lifted by rapturous prayer into the third heaven described by St. Paul and knew that a brother was sick, it would be better to climb down and bring that ailing brother a bowl of soup.

So how do we become ready? *Remember God.* Those who remember God by participating in the ordinary life of the church and acting justly and lovingly toward others will come increasingly to sense the presence of God in their lives. Cunningham suspects that there are many such mystics in the church—young and old people who do not stand out or inspire new movements *but quietly bear witness to an experience of and not just a belief in God.*

Whenever we sense the real presence of God in our hearts, whenever we are made to feel that, as St. Augustine put it, *God is closer to us than we are to ourselves*, then we are on the threshold of true Christian mysticism. This is not to be feared but results in a joy much deeper and more reliable than *happiness* and is the key to being always a free and active follower of Jesus, loving our Father by caring service to neighbors in need.

CHRISTMAS—PLAN B?

An intelligent Catholic woman friend of mine was reminiscing some time ago about her childhood catechism days. Her account of how the Incarnation had been explained left us both amused and sorry. Drawing the picture with a broad brush but with no intended disrespect, the story went like this.

The Father created the world and everything was good. It was supposed to remain that way. All of a sudden Adam *surprised* God by committing sin and, much to his chagrin, God had to go to Plan B. The Father closed the gates of heaven and determined to forget about human beings for a good long time. As years went on, the Son saw men and women muddling about on earth and felt sorry for them. When he first asked the Father if there was anything he could do, the Father told him not to waste his effort. When the Son kept insisting, the Father gave him some conditions to fulfill if he really wanted the gates of heaven opened again.

First of all, he would have to take on a human's miserable nature (shudder!) and live their life. He would also have to endure great suffering on a cross and only then would the Father give in and let them into heaven—almost against his better judgment. We all know how the story turned out.

Does the account seem farfetched and unfair? I have since presented it to well over a hundred adult Catholics and almost all recognize in it their own early training. Where in that story is the compassionate and loving Father? Was an omniscient God really forced into a *Plan B*? Did the Son have to cajole and bargain for our salvation? Did the Father need a *blood sacrifice* to appease his hurt feelings? Is Christmas a time we celebrate the humiliation of the Son who *borrowed* our wretched humanity?

There was no Plan B. From the beginning, God knew there would be sin, but knew as well that his goodness and love would finally triumph. Creation is indeed good because God has always been intimately present in it; deeply involved as the center and ground of the universe which mirrors his infinite richness. Everything not God flows from God and remains in God.

God had always intended that at a moment in time in our history, God would show forth God's centrality and continuous presence in creation. If this was to be done, God had to prepare a suitable *vehicle* for himself—a nature which would, of course, be limited but which must approximate as closely as possible his own divine nature. "Let us make mankind in our own image and likeness" (Gen. 1:26). Though finite (since it was not God himself), human nature was made with a capacity for receiving divine life.

Reflecting on God's plan, master theologian Karl Rahner says, "Man is what God must become if he is ever to become something other than God." And he had decided from all eternity to become something other than God to manifest once and for all the worth of his creation and his intimate participation in it. *The vehicle of human nature was created for the Son who one day would take it to himself.* Meanwhile, we human beings shared the nature which was made for God's Son. This is our ultimate dignity and the key to our worth.

When he took this humanity to himself, Jesus—now man and God—lived it to the full. He did this by developing his gifts and talents in loving relationship with his Father and his neighbor. His goal and delight was unbroken fidelity to love for his Father and fellow human beings. Jesus's total commitment to this love was diminished neither by his being tempted to selfish attractions nor by his experience of intense suffering. *It was by his fidelity to love no matter what* that our redemption was secured. He is both the manifestation of God and the exemplar of genuinely human living.

When in the moral life we speak of Christ as our *model,* we do not mean it as a Little Leaguer might point to a World Series hero. We mean rather that human nature was originally created for the time when Jesus would take it to himself and live it fully as a son of the Father. From that moment on we could be certain there is no other way to be fully human. If even a nonbeliever wishes to live in a truly human way, she or he is bound to the values and self-giving love shown in the life of Christ.

Christmas is not only the feast of *God with us*, it is the affirmation of our human dignity and the sign of how human life must be lived. The One for whom human nature was created has come among us and shows us the only way to live it to the full.

DO IT ANYWAY

On the cusp of a New Year—but for any time we want to break away from limitations or excuses and take another leap into the marvelous freedom God wants us to enjoy—let's open up to some powerful insights offered by St. Teresa of Calcutta:

People are often unreasonable, illogical, and self-centered...
Forgive them anyway.

If you are kind, people may accuse you of selfish, ulterior motives...
Be kind anyway.

If you are successful, you will win some false friends and some true enemies...
Succeed anyway.

If you are honest and frank, people may cheat you...
Be honest and frank anyway.

What you spend years building, someone could destroy overnight...
Build anyway.

If you find serenity and happiness, they may be jealous...
Be happy anyway.

The good you do today, people will often forget tomorrow...
Do good anyway.

Give the world the best you have and it may never be enough...
Give the world the best you've got anyway.

You see, in the final analysis, it is between you and God...
It was never between you and them anyway.

SELF-PLEASURING

I would never title a post "Masturbation"—nor, whenever we get to it, "Fornication." It has been joked that those very words must have been chosen as part of a *fear tactic* to make people flee from such things! Simply as words neither one is neutral, let alone inviting.

By the way, when is the last time you heard them used or anything preached or taught about those topics? I thought so. That is why this reflection carries so much unwanted *baggage* and—probably like the post on "Why Gay?"—stands out like a proverbial *sore thumb* in the list of topics we have seen together. In our society, the heightened climate—confusion, awkwardness, defensiveness and, yes, fear—related to any mention of sexuality has led to my personal decision not to offer parish talks on sexuality for the past ten years. How sad. It's good that other gifts of God have found a warmer welcome.

Many people have asked why it would be such a problem for me to give the basic Church teaching on sexuality and then go on from that. All right, the core teaching of the Church regarding sexuality as I was taught is: *outside of a marital context, any deliberate thought, word, or deed which causes venereal (i.e. sexual) pleasure is a mortal sin.*

Now you want me to take it from there? There is nowhere to take it. That's it. Anything further would be simply to give examples which would be describing the possible types of *mortal sins.* In all fairness to Catholics, for most people, almost all religious treatments of sexuality have been inadequate and unhelpful—terminally impoverished. For now, however, let's just consider *self-pleasuring.*

Many jump to the conclusion that Self-pleasuring always results in *orgasm.* Not so. Though most often solitary, exploring one's body and feelings is, of course, always sexual and often pleasurable. The usual situation is that each human being growing up discovers many aspects of his/her life which are physically, psychologically, or emotionally grounded. Their sexuality includes all these. And it is truly *their* sexuality, not something separate or apart from each individual. They must find out what it means. Each of us needs to discover, explore, *try on, get used to* what it means *for me* to develop into a mature woman or man. What is this body God has given me and why? But looking at the teaching above, that normal and healthy journey will involve and necessitate *deliberate thoughts, words, and deeds which cause sexual pleasure.* That is the way God made us.

Decades of objective inquiries lead psychologists, youth counselors, and, yes, confessors to believe that part of the normal person's development very frequently involves self-pleasuring resulting in orgasm—perhaps 90 percent of males and females. After puberty, this becomes a common and safe way to release tensions arising from physical, emotional, or psychological roots. Very many people carry this long into adulthood and even a satisfying marriage.

As an experienced confessor and pastorally sensitive priest, it is difficult to believe God is pleased with the tiny box into which we have forced a young person's sexual development—surrounded by sin and secrecy, not daring to share questions or discoveries with anyone but a trusted yet equally ignorant peer—frightened by their first ejaculation, *wet dream,* menstruation, or orgasm. These signs of growing up and how God made us should be causes of celebration, not shame. This is part of wholesome human development, not embarking on a life of sin. Even as adults, so many wrongly feel like *second-class citizens* whose practice of self-pleasuring to orgasm must be overcome before God could ever accept anything good from them. Trust that God knows, loves, and keeps in union with God one who lives in hope.

Our core teaching on sexuality, in order to be helpful and correctly understood, demands corrections and clarifications to promote the positive nature of self-discovery by young people growing into their sexuality. They must be supported as they come to know themselves—hormones and weaknesses, how to deal honestly with their needs and wants, how not to *use* others or *be used*—so they can look outward in freedom to find and to give companionship, acceptance, and love. This sinless phase of self-discovery will soon be challenged by a need to be needed ("If you really loved me, you would..."), lying to have sex ("But I really love you, so..."), facing sexual diseases, or the possibility of pregnancy, loss of a good reputation, etc. This is where sin could enter the picture.

There must be (and are) better ways to walk and talk with our children and young people as they (and we) *celebrate* (not be embarrassed by) God's gift of sexuality.

PRAYER OF PETITION

When I was a small boy my family spent its summer vacation in a little town in Maine. One of the most fascinating attractions for me was the local *central office* of the telephone company. The lady who sat at the high dark-wooded switchboard was kind enough to let me watch her crisscross the plugs as she connected party to party through the wondrous invention before her. She was the virtuoso of the switchboard, conducting a symphony of human contacts. People far away from one another were brought close by sharing voices and thoughts, needs, and hopes.

I'm sure the communion of saints is a mystery far too profound to be grasped by simple analogy. Doesn't it seem, though, that God—in whom we all live and move and have our being—is himself the *switchboard* through which we can make vital contact with one another? With those who have died, those who still live on this earth, those separated from us by half the globe, we profess creedal belief that we are all joined together in our one Father and can pray for one another in an effective way. It is God through whom I can direct my prayerful healing love to the child pictured in today's newspaper and who lies starving a continent away. It is God who is our link with one another when distance or other impossibility prevents physical presence. This addresses our first concern regarding *prayer of petition*— how are my love and caring able to touch the other person? Because we are intimately united in God.

The second consideration is much more subtle. Certainly, my prayer for someone in need (even for myself) in no way *reminds* God that a problem exists. A Christian does not pray because she or he feels God is unaware or inattentive to someone's need. I hope we never have the idea that we are more concerned about the person than is God, as though God is holding back aid until God sees whether or not we bother to pray. Those notions are shallow and unworthy of the attentive and unconditioned love of our Father for each of us.

Isn't it more likely that once again we are invited by God to join with him as *co-creators of a redeemed but unfinished world?* Love is a creative force. Just observe the vibrant change in someone who recently has gone from feeling unloved to being loved. Love is a power which bathes and encompasses a person—it heals, it enlivens, it frees.

All prayer of petition is simply a focusing of love. The prayer articulated may be an expression of proper self-love (concern for one's own needs) or of loving care for another. But love—effectively willing the true good of the beloved—is surely the underlying force beneath all our serious petitions in prayer.

Just as all creation in the very beginning resulted from the overflow of God's loving goodness, now we are urged to believe in our mutual union in the Father and focus our co-creative love in prayers of petition for our own and one another's needs and growth. God has made a world in which my love makes a difference and invites me to join my caring with God's. If at times the results of my prayer are not the ones I had anticipated, perhaps I can at least be relieved to know that the kingdom is of more intricate design than my limited vision can perceive. God answers every prayer with "Yes" or "Later" or "I have something better."

For the final question, we turn to philosophy. Here the element of transcendent mystery becomes more acute, for we have no direct experience of *timelessness*. You and I exist in time; God does not. Everything for God is *now*; all eternity is simultaneous. This is why we do not have to imagine a deceased friend waiting in an antechamber of heaven until the month's anniversary Mass is celebrated for her happy repose. It is why I can pray today that the report of last week's biopsy will come back as benign because my co-creative prayer of petition enters the realm of God which is outside of time as we know it. This prayerful focusing of my caring concern already *matters* in the ultimate resolution of the human events at stake.

In the building of the kingdom, God has willed that my love should make a difference. Through the incredible goodness of the timeless God who unites us, my (and your) prayer of petition always matters.

WHAT IS *GOD'S WILL?*

It has happened again. In a scene frequent enough to be classic, I, as priest, walk toward the casket past the milling or seated mourners. There is barely time for me to mumble my quick "I'm very sorry" before the dead child's mother reaches for my hand. "Oh, Father, we know it's God's will but it's so difficult for us…"

That is not the time for theological discussion. But later in my car, I am disheartened by this misunderstanding between God and his people. Contrary to the way that grieving mother understood her words, it was not *God's will* that her little daughter be crushed to death by a truck. He is not a *giant puppeteer* who pulls our strings to cause the events of life. God does not manipulate trucks and little girls because, forgive me, "He loved little Kathy so much God wanted her to go to heaven and be with him." Yet this kind of misunderstanding, admittedly vague and seldom examined in its implications, would suggest just such an *inhumane and selfish God.*

I believe the problem is traceable to the theological distinction between God's *permissive* will and *causal* will. To maintain the fact of God's omnipotence in the creative plan, we have justifiably postulated his *permissive* will—without which nothing can happen in creation. Though it is a profound mystery, we have come rightly to understand that evil, sin, and suffering are indeed permitted by God or they in fact could not exist. This does not mean God likes or approves of them any more than we do. In no way at all need we feel compelled to say that because God knows in advance such evils will happen he therefore causes them. I once witnessed an Alpine skier unknowingly gliding toward a hidden precipice but knowing it in advance did not mean I caused the ensuing deadly fall.

People are given life and sustained in that life, whether they use their freedom to ski unknown trails, or commit sin, or drive down a street where a little girl chases her ball between parked cars.

A friend of mine lost her husband a number of years ago. After a sales trip on his way home to her and their five young children, he fell asleep at the wheel and went over an embankment. He was killed instantly. As far as I know, she has not been to church since that day. She had been told all her life that these things were *God's will*—and she can't feel anything for a God who takes a good man from his loving family. She would never have done such a thing. Nor would you or I *cause* little girls to be killed by trucks as a way to get them to heaven. We could even end up feeling we are better than such a God, more compassionate and loving! Perhaps a combination of inadequate preaching and popular misconceptions has confused her and others into equating God's permissive will with his causal will. Since in daily life we are not familiar with the distinction, people believe God manipulated events to have the tragedy occur. What if the man had been drinking? Did God *inspire* him to drink so he could lose control because *his time had run out?*

We've all experienced someone being warned to take care before an auto trip and heard them shout back "Well, if it's my time to go, there's nothing I can do anyway." This is fatalism, not Christianity. Divine revelation doesn't tell us that careless or not, drunk driving or not, I have X number of days to live. It doesn't say because John developed cancer that God sent it to see how John would react.

I think, in addition, there is a deep and basic need even in mature people to feel that the significant events in their lives are predetermined by *destiny* (or for believers, by God). They are willing, even eager, to forego the reality of personal freedom so long as the ultimate responsibility for what happens doesn't fall on them. It is too unnerving to realize that if Tom had only rested before his wearying drive home, he might be alive today—or that if they had lost some weight, the diabetes or heart attack might not have occurred. But God does not deserve the blame for our own poor judgments or excesses.

Where does God enter the picture? God has been there all along—intimately concerned and present to his people at every moment of their lives. If I, with my limited sense of mercy and compassion, am distraught by children's sufferings and a family's loss, what must be felt by the Christ who wept at his friend Lazarus's tomb?

God is present to sweep up to himself the child who would have been hit by the truck—to make the point strongly—even if there were no God! But there is indeed a loving God who can salvage some good from what would otherwise remain as an absurd and pointless tragedy. The child, the cancer victim, the dead husband are with God in the fullness of life. For those who remain, he invites and urges them to the faith, hope, and trust which can bring healing and solace. God asks them to let him help them become wiser and deeper people in the face of the mystery of suffering, not because God caused it, which he did not, but because in Christ he has been there, too, and can make their personal calvary a prelude to resurrection.

WHITE PRIVILEGE

If, in reading the title, your immediate response is either anger or guilt, then please take a deep breath and relax before continuing! Neither feeling is the purpose of our focus here. On an *up note* for whites, most of us are totally unaware that such privilege exists and, of course, we know that knowledge must always precede any personal culpability.

Wikipedia describes *white privilege* as the advantages enjoyed by white persons beyond what is commonly experienced by nonwhite people in the same social spaces—nation, community, workplace, etc. (It differs from racism or prejudice by the fact that the person benefiting from white privilege need not necessarily hold overt racist beliefs.)

Professor Robert Jensen relates an incident on what white privilege sounds like. "I am sitting in my University of Texas office, talking to a very bright and very conservative white student about affirmative action in college admissions which he opposes and I support. The student says he wants a level playing field with no unearned advantages for anyone. I ask him whether he thinks that in the United States being white has advantages. Have either of us ever benefited from being white in a world run mostly by white people? Yes, he concedes, there is something real and tangible we could call white privilege.

"So, if we live in a world of white privilege—unearned white privilege—how does that affect your notion of a level playing field, I ask. He paused for a moment and said, 'That really doesn't matter.'

"That statement, I suggested to him, reveals the ultimate white privilege—the privilege to acknowledge you have unearned privilege but ignore what it means."

Jensen goes on to reflect on his own life journey as a white in a world of white privilege. "When I seek admission to a university, apply for a job, or hunt for an apartment, I don't look threatening. Almost all the people evaluating me for those things look like me— they are white. The see in me a reflection of themselves, and in a racist world, that is an advantage. I smile. I am white. I am one of them. I am not dangerous. Even when I voice critical opinions, I am cut some slack. After all, I am white. My flaws are more easily forgiven because I am white."

The author James Baldwin once said, "Being white means never having to think about it."

None of this means that whites have a *free pass* to success, fame, or fortune without hard work, consistent application of their talents, and effectively willing what they want themselves to become as persons. Life itself and meaningful accomplishments are easy for precious few people. Individuals can be justly proud and take satisfaction in what good they have done. What our society's provision of white privilege does mean, however, is the obligation for whites to recognize the damaging effects their unasked for but ever-present *empowerment* could have on nonwhites. For anyone who values fairness and believes in the common good of humankind (not to mention the founding goals of our country), reality and truth matter.

We can draw on Professor Peggy McIntosh's years of study on this question. She recognizes that more than a *privilege*, perhaps it is an *over-empowering* of a dominant group. In this short space, let us reflect on her listing of some various conditions upon which whites can count but most of her African American coworkers, friends, and acquaintances cannot depend on:

1) I can, if I wish, arrange to be in the company of people of my own race most of the time;
2) I can avoid spending time with people whom I was trained to mistrust and who have learned to mistrust my kind or me;
3) If I should need to move, I can be pretty sure of renting or purchasing housing in an area which I can afford and in which I would want to live;

4) I can be pretty sure that my neighbors in such a location will be neutral or pleasant to me;

5) I can go shopping alone most of the time, pretty well assured that I will not be followed or harassed;

6) I can do well in a challenging situation without being called *a credit to my race;*

7) Whether I use checks, credit cards, or cash, I can count on my skin color not to work against the appearance of financial reliability;

8) I can arrange to protect my children most of the time from people who might not like them;

9) I do not have to educate my children to be aware of systemic racism for their own daily physical protection;

10) I can swear, or dress in secondhand clothes, or not answer letters without having people attribute these choices to bad morals, the poverty, or illiteracy of my race;

11) I can be pretty sure that if I ask to talk to *the person in charge,* I will be facing a person of my own race;

12) If a traffic cop pulls me over or if the IRS audits my tax return, I can be sure I haven't been singled out because of my race;

13) I can go home from most meetings or organizations I belong to feeling somewhat tied in, rather than isolated, out of place, outnumbered, unheard, held at a distance, or feared;

14) I have no difficulty finding neighborhoods where people approve of our household; and

15) I can think over many options, social, political, imaginative, or professional, without asking whether a person of my race would be accepted or allowed to do what I want to do.

Reality and the truth of what people encounter in their daily lives really do matter. If we have benefited from privilege or empowerment simply because of being white, perhaps we can be more understanding and inclusive of those who haven't. No guilt, just awareness leading to action.

Parents as Children

One of the really challenging things to face in life is when one's parents are noticeably aging—with all that means. So many emotions. And it's not just concern about them—how they take it, their safety, attitudes, worries, health, sense of self. All this brings new concerns and responsibilities for us. It was a long time ago that I started believing that we never fully *grow up* until our parents have died, no matter how much we love them.

I'd like to offer a few specific thoughts that might help people sort out what can easily become severe obstacles to living in the freedom God wants for everyone involved. Would that I could envision and include here every variation of what might arise in situations when one's parents become more like one's children—very much dependent on us; having needs or wants that are not easily met: self-centeredness due to illness, frailty or fear; not being *in charge* anymore; habits of *doing it my way;* forgetting that we, their children, are not really *children* anymore but, according to expectations, have embarked on lives of our own. It's good that *Little House on the Prairie* aired a long time ago because that's rarely the shared experience of today. Life is seldom simple.

+ Modern medicine—and thank God for it—can do wonders. It can also preserve *physical* life when it is obvious to everyone (including or especially the patient) that it's time to move on. That's why *everyone* should have a healthcare agent, designated in writing and witnessed, who is trusted to speak and decide medical treatments if we become incapacitated. Most people do not deal well with their mortality. Death is a part of life, however, and it can be extremely thoughtless for a *patient* not to do everything now in her/his power (healthcare agent, DNR order) to help their loved ones with what will become a difficult time for them.

+ Parents (and the rest of us, too) must always benefit from the respect and care they deserve as human beings. ("Do unto others.") This will not necessarily be easy, and we all have enough experience to know what that implies. It does not mean that every daughter or son who is married (and who perhaps has children at home, with both parents working) can either welcome the parent into their home or spend a disproportionate amount of time attending to the parent's needs. Their own husband/wife and the health of their marriage should be the primary concern. If necessary for a parent's good or the needs of all involved, a nursing home or similar, with caring visits is not *abandonment*.

What patience and trust—on the part of everyone involved—are required to deal well with what is probably for most of them a reality never before imagined or discussed! May the love shown for one another over all the prior years prepare them to cooperate with generosity and understanding.

LIFE'S MEANING: *RELATIONSHIPS*

As much as we might prefer it to be different, there are not many times in life that we can be certain as to God's will or plan. But because we believe truly and deeply that God's wisdom is revealed in sacred scripture—especially in the words of Jesus—we do indeed have some security in turning to that source for direction. There it is clear that God created us in a way that *the meaning of human life is relationship.*

Responding to a scribe's question, Jesus said, "You shall love the Lord your God with all your heart, with all your soul, with all your mind, and with all your strength... You shall love your neighbor as yourself. There is no other commandment greater than these" (Mk. 13:30–31).

Love has been defined as *effectively willing the true good of the other. Effectively willing*": not merely wishing, or hoping, or some general good will but doing whatever is reasonably in your power to foster the other's *true good* (which they might not yet even recognize as good for them); *the other* refers to *love your neighbor as yourself.* Only one place does Jesus give the necessary and most important criterion for each person's salvation (and it involves *effective action*): "Come you who are blessed by my Father... For I was hungry and you gave me food...a stranger and you welcomed me...naked and you clothed me...ill and you cared for me...whatever you did for one of these least brothers of mine, you did for me" (Mt. 25:31–46).

It is also clear, expressed by St. Paul, that *love* continues when we pass through the doorway we refer to as *death* into the next phase of human life. *Faith* yields to face-to-face union with God, and *hope* ends with possession. "At present I know partially; then I shall know fully as I am fully known. So faith, hope, and love remain…but the greatest of these is love…love never ends" (1 Cor. 13:12–13, 8).

There are three necessary and crucial focuses of our love—our caring and effective attention: *self* ("love your neighbor as your self"), *others* (Scripture tells us *everyone* is my neighbor, beloved by God), and *God*. We must remember that this *love* does not always or necessarily involve pleasant emotions or *warm fuzzies*. If that were essential, Jesus could never *command* us to love everyone. It's possible we might not even *like* them, so long as we are effectively doing what we can for their true good. It's why Jesus could tell us to love even our enemies. But all true love (even of self) creates and involves us in a *relationship*—emotionally pleasant or not. According to God, love is what makes us human and fulfills in us God's gift of life. *The meaning of human life is relationship.*

UNCOMFORTABLE FACTS

I'd like to share with you a letter to the Editor of the *NCR* (Feb. 3, 2012), written by an orthodox and respected Catholic theologian. It helps advance our search to find the freedom God wants for us because "the truth will set you free" (Jn. 8:32).

"As a theologian, I appreciated your coverage of tensions between the hierarchy and the academy in your Christmas issue. In removing women's ordination from discussion, the pope and bishops have to deny historical facts, such as ordination of women in the early Middle Ages. [*Diaconate, part of the sacrament of Holy Orders*]

"History is filled with uncomfortable facts—or the lack of them. For example, many Catholics believe that transubstantiation is a doctrine that all must believe. As a matter of fact, however, transubstantiation is not a doctrine but a theory proposed to explain the real presence of Christ in the Eucharist. Other explanations are possible.

"To be a doctrine of faith, a religious belief must be proclaimed to be such by an ecumenical council or by a pope speaking ex cathedra as head of the church. Neither transubstantiation nor the inability of women to be ordained meets this high standard. The same is true of moral doctrines, such as the sinfulness of artificial contraception.

"If the standard is lowered to something like the common teaching of the church over a long period of time, then Catholic faith would have to include the morality of slavery and the immorality of charging interest on loans. The sacramentality of marriage is a Catholic doctrine, yet Christians were able to divorce for centuries and there was no Catholic wedding ritual before the twelfth century.

"Facts are the rocks upon which many beliefs get dashed. But they are also the foundation of a solid—if not always conventional—faith."

Prof. Joseph Martos (Louisville, Kentucky)

LENT—ALL ONE NEEDS

From the beginning of Isaiah:58, "'God… Why do we fast and you do not see it, afflict ourselves and you take no note of it?'

"On your fast day you carry out your own pursuits… Yes, your fast ends in quarreling and fighting, striking with wicked claw. Would that today you might fast so as to make your voice heard on high! Is this the manner of fasting I wish, of keeping a day of penance: That a man bow his head like a reed and lie in sackcloth and ashes? Do you call this a fast, a day acceptable to the Lord?

"This rather is the fasting that I wish: releasing those bound unjustly, untying the thongs of the yoke; Setting free the oppressed, breaking every yoke; Sharing your bread with the hungry, sheltering the oppressed and the homeless; Clothing the naked when you see them, and not turning your back on your own. Then your light shall break forth like the dawn, and your wound shall quickly be healed; Your vindication shall go before you, and the glory of the Lord shall be your rear guard. Then you shall call, and the Lord will answer, you shall cry for help, and he will say: *Here I am!*"

Responding to Isaiah for our times, these following observations could help us not simply *to give something up* but develop and solidify a mind-set to *change our hearts* during Lent. This important key to a true Lent is adapted from Fr. Richard Rohr, a treasured spiritual guide and founder of the Center for Action and Contemplation, offers powerful insights into what is *really* our Catholic *tradition:*

"In many recent elections, one would have thought that homosexuality and abortion were the new litmus tests of Christianity. Where did this come from? They never were the criteria of proper membership for the first 2000 years, but reflect very recent culture wars instead—and largely from people who think of themselves as *traditionalists!* The fundamentals were already resolved in the early Apostles' Creed and Nicene Creed. Note that none of the core beliefs are about morality at all. The Creeds were more mystical, cosmological, and about aligning our lives inside of a huge sacred story. *When you lose the mystical level, you always become moralistic as a cheap substitute.*

"Jesus is clearly much more concerned about issues of pride, injustice, hypocrisy, blindness and what I have called *The Three Ps* of power, prestige, and possessions, which are probably 95 percent of Jesus's written teaching. We conveniently ignore this 95 percent to concentrate on a morality that usually has to do with human embodiment. That's where people get righteous, judgmental, and upset, for some reason. The body seems to be where we carry our sense of shame and inferiority, and early-stage religion has never gotten much beyond these *pelvic* issues. As Jesus puts it, 'You ignore the weightier matters of the law—justice, mercy, and good faith…and instead you strain out gnats and swallow camels' (Mt. 23:23–24). We worry about what people are doing in bed much more than making sure everybody has a bed to begin with. There certainly is a need for a life-giving (and *joy*-giving) sexual morality, but one could question whether Christian societies have found it yet.

"Christianity will regain its moral authority when it starts emphasizing social sin in equal measures with individual (read *body-based*) sin and weaves them both into a seamless garment of love and truth."

THE CATHOLIC CHURCH
AND CONTRACEPTION

Very briefly, let us distinguish between contraception and *abortion*. Abortion is the deliberate expulsion from the womb of a nonviable fetus, thereby causing its death. In light of current scientific/philosophical knowledge, it is commonly assumed that human life begins at *conception* (the union of sperm and ovum). Once that has happened and given the normal/usual developmental progression, a human birth will take place in about nine months. No one can be sure with certainty that there is any other point between conception and birth where one could say "only at this time human life begins." If it could be *definitively determined* that human life began only, say, a week or six weeks after conception, then we all should—and I hope would—accept that. Without that currently nonexisting certitude, most responsible people would grant that human life begins at conception—with all the respect and rights due to *innocent human life* that religions and society wish to accord. Further, this would suggest that abortion is much more a *human rights issue* than a *medical ethics issue*.

When we begin considering *artificial contraception* (i.e., not simply restricting intercourse to nature's own periodic female infertility), then mechanical, chemical, physical, or medical means are some ways used to prevent conception. Almost all those means prevent the union of sperm and ovum resulting in conception. To be extremely careful, the only method to be treated uniquely is the IUD (intrauterine device) which may in some cases prevent a *fertilized* ovum from implanting in the uterus. If human life begins at conception (fertilization), then this would be *abortive*, not contraceptive.

[*Please bear with me.* It is most important to understand the above as prelude to what I will be suggesting for your consideration—i.e., that abortion must continue to be seen as the very serious wrong of taking an innocent human life—but that abortion is *essentially different* from artificial contraception which does *not* destroy human life! Fertilization has not yet occurred. I suggest that the inadequate ways Church teachers have presented abortion and artificial contraception both as very serious evils have led to people's confusion and frustration. This has promoted neither understanding nor freedom nor virtue.]

Pope Paul VI ("On Human Life," 1968) taught essentially: "It is necessary that each and every marriage act remain ordered *per se* to the procreation of human life." The *Catholic Catechism for Adults* confirms, "Each and every sexual act in a marriage needs to be open to the possibility of conceiving a child" (chapter 30). Church teaching says that artificial contraception interferes with that goal so is to be regarded as seriously wrong. Some bishops and a few theologians have attempted to claim the teaching is *infallible,* but it meets none of the traditionally accepted criteria for such certitude and nonreformability. (Indeed, Pope Paul VI's selected public presenter of his letter, Fr. F. Lambruschini, said to those assembled that the matter was still open for further discussion—which statement was widely circulated and was never denied or clarified by the Pope.)

Over the many years since the Pope's restatement of that teaching, it is a historical fact that many committed Catholic theologians have dissented from it, and vast numbers of married practicing Catholics have used artificial contraception at some time in their marriage. Confessors know that in the past few decades the prohibition has become for many people a nonissue. *Responsible parenthood* is also a firm Church teaching—i.e., do not bring into the world more children than you can properly raise. When faced with a dilemma of having to choose between the sexual expression of their mutual love (called *graced* in Church teaching) and responsible parenthood, the faithful very often chose contraception as less of an *evil.* From some couples' testimony, their conviction that they could not responsibly have another child at this time led to using contraception because they would never want to be in a situation where they might contemplate taking a human life by an abortion.

Much of the theological/pastoral dissent comes from those who are convinced that the teaching *each and every sexual act in marriage must always be open to procreation* is excessively biologistic, a misstatement of natural law, or *impersonally act-centered* rather than *person-centered*. Some add that the teaching is, at the very least, a sadly confusing overstatement of what is otherwise a truly valuable goal—reminding people to avoid a *contraceptive_mentality*. That seductive trap could foster in some a self-absorption by which the couple is unwilling to share their love and life even with their own future children. Difficult to believe for those who welcome children, it is nonetheless a pitfall in our affluent culture.

It is a freely chosen and complex *philosophical/theological reasoning process* by which Church teachers have come to the conclusions offered above. They have articulated many high and worthwhile *ideals*—mutual love expressed sexually, responsible parenthood, never separating the act's dual purposes of holy sexual love and openness to procreation, etc. For married couples (or for anyone not well trained in that precise reasoning process), it would still demand considerable understanding and trust, mature holiness, and self-direction for a couple to embrace all those conclusions as their own. If faced with what they, in prayerful conscience, consider truly impossible for them to achieve all the goals—frustration, bewilderment at these demands of the Church, self-deprecation, and alienation could easily follow. These decisions are made as the couple experiences daily the challenges of growing together, even though the spouses well may differ in maturity, intelligence and understanding, personal needs, and depth of faith. At the same time, they are facing the demands of making a living, raising a family, coping with limitations, illness, obligations toward their parents, etc. Church teachers and leaders are called not only to urge us toward the ideals but also to employ the language, explanations, and dialog so as not to put "heavy burdens on people's shoulders...and not lift a finger to move them" (Mt. 23:3)?

I would so love to see Church teachers issue a pastoral/spiritual letter reminding the faithful that even trying one's very best does not guarantee that someone at every moment is always able to achieve any given ideal—or even less, a set of ideals. Affirm that *when I, as a Catholic, listen to Church teachings and the Jesus I know from Scripture and prayer and then I generously decide what is truly the best I can do here and now, I am committing no sin.* After all, isn't that what we teach *must always be followed* as a fully informed *conscience?*

Addendum:

Once, while celebrating the Sacrament of Reconciliation, a young single person confessed as two sins: having sex and using a condom. (A sad but not unexpected result of the *keep all the rules* mentality.) First, the immorality would lie in the inappropriate nature of a sexual but uncommitted relationship. The Church's concern with artificial contraception has to do with the twofold nature of marital sexuality—deepening mutual love in a way that is open to procreation. *Unprotected* premarital sex might very possibly result in pregnancy, and then an abortion taking a human life. In this context, a condom might prevent a greater evil, not cause a *second* sin.

TOUGHER BEING YOUNG

I doubt if being young, at least from six years old onward, was ever easy. We all needed whatever help we could get, whether we wanted it or not! But I find myself today praying with greater intensity than ever for young people. So many I've been blessed to know personally, and they are good!

Every generation has had to face its own challenges in growing up. Almost everyone had growing pains from some or all of the usual—self-doubt, uncertainty in relationships, bullying (though less widespread than today), sex, drugs/alcohol, school, etc. Today, however, we have to add to that list even more difficult changes that are part of our culture.

Before continuing, let me make it clear that I am not a *world hater.* I also believe that with the help of God's Spirit, people can overcome even the worst obstacles. TV and the news bring us their stories, and they are amazingly humbling and inspiring. But that doesn't mean we should turn a blind eye to things like: 1) the lack of heroes (we used to find them in sports, politics, even business—think about those areas for a moment); 2) problems in the Church (where we easily trusted our leadership and clergy for wisdom and help); 3) increased dysfunction in many family settings (making no judgments on individuals, but facing that many parents are *not there* in the way their children need); 4) the almost complete disappearance of the *Catholic culture* (the personal security and well-being from knowing one is always part of and supported by Christ and his people—one's parish faith-community; 5) the disappearance of *manners* (really a basic respect and caring for other people); and 6) the widespread acceptance of *cheating* (school and business).

Driving along a beautiful country lane on a perfect summer day, I passed a young fellow on his bike—and on a cell phone. I feared a total disconnect from nature and his life-giving surroundings. Had he just come from home and a few hours in his room playing an interactive game? Aren't one's primary interactions supposed to be with people? Is text messaging any substitute for face-to-face hanging out, kidding, and sharing with live friends? Do my iPod earpieces lead to a further isolation—walled inside myself? Some of today's tough challenges for our really great kids. Be there for them, love them—tell them! They deserve it.

Good Friday/Divorce

"It was all over. All the bright promise of what might have been was gone. The hopeful words were silenced and the beautiful messages of love seemed so far away. It was going to be a wonderful life—what an adventure it was to have been! Our expectations were so great and now our hopes lie dead before us. How can life bring such a cruel surprise? Is there nothing left?"

What have you just read about, my friend? Was it a description of Calvary's desolation on Good Friday? It could so easily have been. The friends of Jesus endured every one of those emotions; felt keenly the pain of losing their Beloved. Nothing could have convinced them that all was not finished; there was no way for the face of hope to be seen. Every plan they had made vanished on the tree of crucifixion.

But the description was not of Calvary at all—at least, not Christ's calvary. Read it again. Doesn't it sound familiar? Haven't you lived through every word of it when married life slipped away? "Could there be two Calvaries—Christ's and mine?" Is it cruel to remind you that what you ask is true; that you and Christ have shared so intimately? I had to remind you how utterly hopeless that first Calvary appeared to all who lived through it. There was no way they could see any good springing from such pain and loss. There was no reason for living another day because the meaning of life had ended for them.

But what happened? Resurrection! Unexpected new life breaking forth from darkness and death. How totally unexpected, how unbelievable—but how true! Forgive me for reminding you of your own calvary, but it was the only way to remind you of your own resurrection. It's so impossible to believe—and you don't know when or how it's coming, what form it will take. Just like the first one! But our Father loves us too much to permit calvaries to be unanswered by resurrections.

(May I share a poem I came across and with which
I am very taken? It says a lot from and about an
Easter Woman and an Easter *Woman*.)

Lord, Make Me an Easter Woman

My journey begins on Good Friday.
Would I be there even though I couldn't bear the thought?
Would I follow Him down the dusty road as He bore the cross
Or would I run ahead, over and over, so He could see me?
What should I do? I don't want to make it worse for Him.
Would I hide in the crowd, afraid for myself?
Would I weep regardless of what anyone thought?
Would I crumple to the ground unable to go on
Once I realized I could not save Him?
Oh my God, how would I act at Calvary?
Would I watch as the nails went in?
Would I cover my ears from the clang of hammer meeting nail?
What if He screamed? Could I take it? Could I be strong?
Would I vomit? Would I faint? Would I despair?
Would I break down and ask His Father to save Him?
To change His plan? Who needs this stupid plan?
Why should a good man have to suffer for mankind's sins?
This plan is imperfect and not worthy of God.
The Father can do anything. He needs nothing. Why this painful
    plan?
Would I tell God I hate Him for this? Will I ever understand?
And what of His mother and the other women? They are suffering,
    too!
Did His mother say "Yes" to His Father only to pay such an awful
    price?
This is love? This is crazy! Would I really think that? Or would I
    understand?
Would I say "I can't take it anymore" and leave, deserting Him?

And if I stayed, would I be relieved when He drew His last breath?
Would I abandon all hope or decide to stay the course?
Even if I didn't fully understand the course.
Then when they took down His body, would I still be there?
Would I collapse in sorrow? Would I pray?
Would I go home for a rest? Where was home?
At Sabbath's end, would I sprint to be near Him again?
Would I fall to my knees weeping when I see the empty space?
Would I see the angels? Would I know them?
Would I see Jesus? Would I recognize Him?
Would I do a little dance or let out a happy cry
When the first glimmer of hope coursed through my body?
If I am the one He asks to go tell the others,
Would I ask Him to come with me? Reluctant to face the men alone?
Why would Jesus speak to a woman first?
And when He ascends forty days later,
Would I be angry at Him for abandoning me to them?
I was with Him all the way. I was faithful to the end.
Now would I be told not to worry my pretty little head?
They would take it from here.

IT'S MY TURN!

The whole point of our journey together is to become more free of the almost countless obstacles from unnecessary external constraints, internal desires or fears, and even wrong or incomplete understanding of what we think is *God's will.* Only one thing will really help us in our search for the freedom God wants for each of us. Jesus said, "The truth will set you free" (Jn. 8:32). So let's see if analyzing a not uncommon attitude will help us better to enjoy more moments of daily life—being understanding and affirming, not *grouchy.*

A good number of years ago, an upstate priest classmate asked me if he could bring to the shore for a few days' vacation two brothers from the high school where he was chaplain. My friend had been close to their family, and an alcoholic father had abandoned them all about eight years before. Now Jim was eighteen, and Chris had just turned fifteen, though there is never a *right age* to face such a rough situation.

They were great young guys and had really loved the one time they had experienced swimming in ocean surf. So we headed for an overnight at a cottage someone loaned me. *Like ducks to water* is the phrase that comes to mind to describe the exuberant chaos that ensued. After a lot of horseplay between the brothers, Chris sneaked up on his older brother and managed to *de-pants* him! (If you don't remember middle school gym days, it is exactly what it sounds like.) Jim—three years older, more reserved, and *sophisticated*—had a fit and screamed at his brother, "Grow up, you jerk!" Chris was hooting and laughing as he swam over to me and said, "But it's *my turn!*" I have never forgotten that phrase.

It was *his turn*…to be an annoying younger brother, perhaps to get back at Jim for a time Jim had embarrassed him, or just to act like

53

a *nut* to *let out all the stops,* to draw attention, who knows? Over the years, haven't we all seen things that other people (usually younger ones) do or say or *act like* that led us to make a disparaging or judgmental comment? Here I'm speaking not of immoral or criminal or truly destructive behavior. Just stuff like revving up an unmuffled car or motorcycle simply to get attention, piercings, or wearing clothes that don't meet our *approval,* being *too loud* at times—just not as *proper* as I would like them to be.

I'm suggesting that: 1) we aren't the *culture police* who has to censure and comment on everything that anyone does (especially younger people who *try on* behaviors, attitudes, or *styles* in their effort to be regarded by peers as *cool,* while they are trying to decide who they want to be when they *grow up*); and 2) instead of becoming *grouchy* with a whole generation or two who were born after we were, we should just *chill* more—meaning, freely to let go of the things that aren't worth our *disapproval* or snarky comment. As people who should enjoy each day being alive, let's interact, affirm, and chuckle with those who are simply taking *their turn.* Let's not forget that some years ago, we had *our turn!*

DYING: *YOUR* PLAN

As a Catholic moralist committed to your freedom in God, I had planned to offer some important thoughts about transitioning from this phase of our life into the arms of God—or what we call the dying process. *Please read this rather lengthy post, and you won't be sorry. I find it better than I could do, yet I can endorse every word of it—and I hope it helps you formulate* your *plan. [Susan Jacoby, "Taking Responsibility for Death."* (New York Times, *March 31, 2012)*

I was standing by my eighty-nine-year-old mother's hospital bed when she asked a doctor, "Is there anything you can do to give me back the life I had last year when I wasn't in pain every minute?" The young medical resident, stunned by the directness of the question, blurted out, "Honestly, ma'am, no."

And so, Irma Broderick Jacoby went home and lived another year, during which she never again entered a hospital or subjected herself to an invasive, expensive medical procedure. The pain of multiple degenerative diseases was eased by prescription drugs, and she died last November after two weeks in a hospice on terms determined by explicit legal instructions and discussions with her children—no respirators, no artificial feeding, no attempts to buy one more day for a body that would not let her turn over in bed or swallow without agony.

The hospice room and pain-relieving palliative care cost only about $400 a day, while the average hospital stay costs Medicare over $6,000 a day. Although Mom's main concern was her comfort and dignity, she also took satisfaction in not running up Medicare payments for unwanted treatments and not leaving private medical bills for her children to pay. A third of the Medicare budget is now spent in the last year of life, and a third of that goes for care in the last month. Those figures would surely be lower if more Americans, while they were still healthy, took the initiative to spell out what treatments they do—and do not—want by writing living wills and appointing health care proxies.

As the aging baby boom generation places unprecedented demands on the health care system, there is little ordinary citizens can do to influence either the cost or the quality of the treatment they receive. However, end-of-life planning is one of the few actions within the power of individuals who wish to help themselves and their society. Too few Americans are shouldering this responsibility.

Of course, many people want more aggressive treatment than my mother. But advance directives aren't *death panels*; they can also be used to ensure the deployment of every tool of modern medicine. They can be changed or withdrawn at any time by a mentally competent person.

But public opinion polls consistently show that most Americans, like my mother, worry about too much rather than too little medical intervention. In a Pew Research Center poll released in 2006, only 22 percent said a doctor should always try to save a patient's life, while 70 percent believed that patients should sometimes be allowed to die. More than half said they would tell their doctor to end treatment if they were in great pain with no hope of improvement.

Yet only 69 percent had discussed end-of-life care with a spouse; just 17 percent, or 40 percent of those over sixty-five, had done so with their children. One-third of Americans had a living will and even fewer have taken the more legally enforceable measure of appointing a health care proxy to act on their behalf if they cannot act for themselves.

The latter omission is especially disturbing because by 2030, more than 8.5 million Americans will be over eighty-five—an age at which roughly half will suffer from Alzheimer's disease or some other form of irreversible dementia. For many members of the baby boom generation—more likely to be divorced and childless than their parents—there may be no legal next of kin.

Without advance directives, even a loving child may be ignorant of her parent's wishes. My mother remained conscious and in charge of her care until just a few days before she died, but like most women over eighty-five, she was a widow. My younger brother died of pancreatic cancer two weeks before she did. It was an immense comfort to me at a terrible time to have no doubts about what she wanted.

My mother drew up her directives in the 1980s when she was a volunteer in the critical care lounge of her local hospital. She once watched, appalled, as an adult daughter threw a coffeepot at her brother for suggesting that their comatose mother's respirator be turned off. Because the siblings could not agree and the patient had no living will, she was kept hooked up to machines for another two weeks at a cost (then) of nearly $80,000 to Medicare and $20,000 to her family, even though her doctors agreed there was no hope.

The worst imaginable horror for my mother was that she might be kept alive by expensive and painful procedures when she no longer had a functioning brain. She was equally horrified by the idea of family fights around her deathbed. "I don't want one of you throwing a coffeepot at the other," she told us in a half joking, half serious fashion.

There is a clear contradiction between the value that American society places on personal choice and Americans' reluctance to make their own decisions insofar as possible about the care they will receive as death nears. Obviously, no one likes to think about sickness and death. But the politicization of end-of-life planning and its entwinement with religion-based culture wars provide extra irrational obstacles to thinking ahead when it matters most.

As someone over sixty-five, I do not consider it my duty to die for the convenience of society. I do consider it my duty to myself and younger generations to follow the example my mother set by doing everything in my power to ensure that I will never be the object of medical intervention that cannot restore my life but can only prolong a costly living death.

Making Freer Kids

If you have kids who are quite young or perhaps not so young, I wanted to share some approaches which will help them become *more free*. In all honesty, I use some of these methods with adults, with only minor changes. After all, do any of us ever *grow up* completely?

Resist the Urge to Deny Or Dismiss Feelings

Ineffective parental responses to children's feelings include "I'm hot" "It's not hot, it's cold. Keep your sweater on" "I'm tired" "You couldn't be tired, you just napped" "It hurts" "It doesn't hurt. It's just a little scratch." A better way to respond would acknowledge the child. In response to "It hurts," the parent should say "Sometimes even a tiny little scratch can be painful. Let me see it." That kind of talk is deeply respectful and nurtures relationships.

Replace Threats with Choices

We all love to make our own choices. Instead of a parent saying, "If you play with that water gun in the living room once more, I'll..." Mom or Dad should say, "Not in the living room. Let's see, where can you play with that? I guess you can play with it in the bathroom or maybe outdoors. You decide." Suddenly, the child is in charge. Be sure the choices are options that are acceptable to you so whichever the child picks, you're satisfied.

Encourage Your Child to Find Solutions

Don't immediately try to fix your child's problems. When the kids ask parents for advice, they've already been thinking about possible solutions—and you want them to keep on working it through. By treating them as problem-solvers, that's what they'll become. Suggest the child make a list of possible ways to address a problem, writing down even the most outlandish or ridiculous ideas. Then they cross them off one by one to reach an acceptable conclusion. Though you're itching to give them advice, wait until they've really explored it as much as they can. Then you can say, "Here's what I think. I don't know if this will be comfortable for you or if it makes sense to you, but you might want to consider…"

Use Humor

This works especially well with younger kids. "You can yell at a kid, you can hit a kid, you can insist or threaten—and you will get nowhere. But use a little bit of humor, and the kids are ready to respond." For instance, use a British accent. Or a vampire voice. "Change the mood, and they're all imitating you." And cooperating.

Write It Down

"There are some things you can write in a note that you can't really say easily because kids will tune you out." You can give your thoughts to a child to read on his/her own. You can even use this with children who can't read yet—you can recite your note to them. Somehow, seeing something in writing makes kids take the words more seriously.

All this respects them, helps communication, and moves them forward. Good luck!

Happily Ever After?

Ultimately, yes.

But on this side of passing through the doorway we call death? For most human beings, life is not a *fairy tale* and will not every moment be *happy* or without serious challenges, setbacks, burdens, disappointments—even tragedy. Lest we misunderstand, however, or get depressed by this, let me begin at the...end.

To know Scripture at all (God's own personal words to us) is to know that each of us is made in the *image and likeness of God*. So many times we are told in clear and certain terms that "God first loved us" (we didn't have to ask to be noticed!), God calls each of us by name as God's children, Jesus says we are not God's *slaves* but *friends*, with such constant attention paid to us that *the hairs on our head are counted, whatever you ask Me shall be given to you,* and endless more pledges of eternal love, affection, unlimited aid through the presence of the Spirit bringing wisdom, forgiveness, and healing—all God's unconditional love, not based on any response from us. Madness? No, that's how God has chosen to love us.

Think for a moment about natural disasters, the horrors of war, the suffering of innocent and good people, innocent children dying of a terrible disease or being hurt or neglected by the very people they love. Those tragedies are known philosophically as *the problem of evil* (Why does an all-powerful and totally loving God tolerate evil in the creation God chose?) and make us all wonder. Even saints have searched and prayed to know a satisfying answer to that question. There is no known explanation of which we can be certain. But are there *hints?*

Even God accepted in Christ: wretched suffering, rejection, and great physical and psychological pain, and even passed through death on the way to the new and endless life of resurrection. Most evil and horror comes from what people inflict on others or themselves; it is never from God, God's desire, or God *testing us*. God respects our *freedom of choice*, given to each of us as an invitation to co-create with God but that we can selfishly turn to things which will destroy. Are there *hints* as to the possibility of some good coming from the existence of evil? We see or read about so many examples of how human beings have achieved great personal growth, moral strength, virtue, and holiness through standing up to or accepting/integrating powerful challenges or personal suffering. Even more wonderful is that, from vast and broad studies of people in many cultures and societies, we can validly assume that countless millions are achieving that same greatness in the silence of their ordinary lives.

Let me simply say I have never met or heard of anyone who did not have some painful challenges or suffering in her/his life. Do we know it from them? Very often, no. And that we do not see it in their lives is part of their very generous, admirable, and deliberate achievement. It is not shame or fear or despair that keeps them from exposing to us their burdens, it is their kindness, humility, and holiness, whether they are *believers* or not. Is another *hint* of goodness that so many go the *extra mile* with patience and compassion, creating space and support for one another—as we each try to *fill in the holes* which evil has brought into our lives?

Certain branches of Orthodox Christians believe that, in the end, everyone will be *saved*. This is not part of the common Christian tradition. Some hope might come from the fact of God's incredible love for all God's children, the incomprehensible wisdom and power of God (which could, perhaps, beyond any human understanding, *reconcile opposites* or *irresistibly attract a person's freedom by God's unconditioned love*)—but such a conclusion can in no way be certain and remains total mystery. Only a fool would live a sinful and selfish life based on an assumption that *everyone will be saved*. If our hearts and love are wide enough, however, we could still hope for every fellow human being that, indeed, since *nothing is impossible for God*, somehow everyone—after being enlightened and purified—would personally benefit from Jesus's loving redemption. Though we don't know how or if, God's incomprehensible mercy—undeserved by all—might provide an unexpected but more complete *happily ever after.*

GREAT EXPECTATIONS

How much is a single person capable of? And groups of people? Such as bishops, congress, a supreme court? Let's take a moment to review our usually unspoken but often underlying *great expectations*—of all those who are chosen to be our leaders—popes and presidents, too. We think, *But the Cardinals chose him* or *We elected him.* And did that make any one *more than a single person*? "When pricked, does he not bleed?"

In our contemporary age, no matter how intelligent, informed, or *graced* one is, a single person cannot begin to fathom the complexity and extent of developments, events, interactions, possibilities, challenges: a twenty-four-hour news cycle bringing instant information from all over the world, political awakenings or repression, natural disasters, a global economy that few seem truly to understand, the growth of knowledge and its best expression (words can always be improved upon!), universal yearnings for freedom, peace, security, respect. All these and *sinfulness*, too! Hatred, jealousy, greed, lying and duplicity, arrogance, desire to control and subjugate—and so on. It is simply common sense that even presidents and popes, congress, and justices, and bishops need broad consultation, honest discussion, with humility and discernment, to be free enough to overcome the many obstacles to fuller truth. And the higher the position, not the least obstacle is often *the way we have always done it.*

Perhaps the problems are not so much *unsolvable* as *overwhelming*. Feel better? We should because there's a big difference. Human beings are *very* resilient. But we can only bring to bear wisdom, courage, hope, reasoning, even faith—if we have time to breathe. Just as important are *realistic expectations*—requiring sometimes serious or even radical reevaluation of political structures, religious beliefs, and cultural practices, and seeing whether all our *leaders*, secular and religious, are being faithful to their *job descriptions*. Most of us human beings are positive, hopeful, and patient to a point. Perhaps our *great expectations* could even become part of the *solution*, but not if those expectations are taken for granted, unexamined, or unrealistic.

Within the lifetime of so many among us today, people did indeed *take it for granted* that most politicians were, at heart, well-meaning, trustworthy, and could handle the job. Congress, for the most part, would put the needs of the country and its citizens before partisan advantage. The supreme court would put justice and fairness ahead of personal politics or ideology. Bishops lived the Gospel responsibly by service, a welcoming inclusion, humility, and compassion. These were all part of the *culture* and *job descriptions* we counted on.

In recent times, many people have come to the conclusion that we, as citizens or churchgoers, can no longer be sanguine that all those in the various authorities can be counted on to live up to the expectations we have afforded them. Let us remember there is only One Savior, Jesus, who—with the Father and Spirit are God—and everyone else is *human* (with all the potential *good* and *evil* that brings). Of course, we can and should have *great expectations* of one another, and often they have been justified. Just *no guarantees!* With eyes wide open, let us pray.

MY FRIEND THE SPIRIT

When you were younger and first heard *doctrines* about God and Jesus, did you ever think that you would someday be *friends?* I mean, real friends who could *hang out* together, share secrets, and be there for one another, really be understood and *always accepted just as we are?* I doubt it. But that is exactly how God wants to interact with each and every one of us.

Even loving parents, for good measure, often portrayed God as the *ultimate policeman*—and because God sees *everything,* we quickly realized as kids that we didn't stand a chance. If we did something wrong, nowhere to hide! (Belated apologies to policemen and to God. Neither of them deserve that burden since they are there only to help us, not *catch us.*)

Jesus told his apostles (and us) before he ascended to his Father that he would be with us all days. Which is how we can speak with him anytime we want and walk through life together. But we should spend a few minutes realizing how he planned to help us and other people keep growing, healing, and hoping: "The Advocate, the Holy Spirit, whom the Father will send in my name, will teach you everything, and remind you of all I have said to you" (Jn. 14:26). "The love of God has been poured into our hearts through the Spirit of God dwelling within us" (Rom. 5,:5 and 8,:11) Even though we can't quite believe we're good enough to merit all that attention and help, the appropriate response for each of us is "Wow!"

My purpose today is to talk about my friend, the Holy Spirit. So far as the Spirit is concerned, She wants each of us continually to interact with Her as trusted *friends*—though we might have to spend some time thinking about how that works. [By the way, the other two Persons in God—the Father and the Son, Jesus—are known, for obvious reasons, as *He*. Spirits have no *gender*, so better to reflect both of the human genders made in God's image and likeness. I prefer to use *She* for the Holy Spirit.]

St. Paul was a good Jew, raised with a tremendous respect for the written Law of Moses which the Jews saw as another great gift of God to help people know how to live as God's faithful children. But after the full mystery and truth of Jesus became known, Paul told all followers of Jesus that "You are not under the Law, but under *grace*" (Rom. 6:14). Grace is never some *thing* but the living presence of God (or the presence of the Spirit, the Advocate, *who will teach you everything*). To put it forcefully, if one were always attuned to and following the guidance of the Spirit, one would never need to hear about God's *written Law*. However, for almost everyone, the *external* Law is a useful if not truly necessary reminder of the *interior* guidance of the Spirit.

Learn to recognize the interaction each of us has with the Spirit—*develop a conscious awareness of when this is happening!* Let's take some examples of how it happens, and then add your personal ones. We have heard a certain scripture reading or offered a specific prayer a hundred times—and the next time a *light bulb* turns on in our mind and *we know a deeper meaning than we had ever imagined!* As priests, many times we've had someone tell us that something they heard us say in a homily or in confession changed their life or gave them such hope—and we are sure we never said such a thing. But the Spirit did. Or we listen to a friend's problem wanting to help and come up with a thought or approach which amazes us how we could ever have thought of that advice. Or something on the news or TV reminds us of a person or situation we have been avoiding and we realize that right now is the time to do something.

These events are not *chance* or *coincidence*. We must see with new eyes how the Spirit is interacting with us. The Belgian Cardinal Suenens, a holy leader in the charismatic movement, reflects, "As death approaches, I see on every page of my life a watermark, so to speak, that shows how the attentive love of God has watched over my daily goings and comings, so much is it true that what we called chance or coinciding circumstances were but God's Spirit at work with infinite delicacy."

How Do I Come Across?

In the early eighties, a book was published that became very popular because it struck a chord with lots of people, *Men are from Mars, Women are from Venus*. Although some differences between the genders are quite evident, this went much deeper into the topic. TV sitcoms find many laughs in the fact that women or men can literally be *stereotyped* by their predictably different reactions to the same problem or event.

But let's take a broader look at how *people in general* can differ from one another, sometimes affecting their whole outlook on life. What about *optimists* and *pessimists?* They can be of either gender and, despite their outlook, can work at becoming balanced and even *holy*. But it certainly helps to know more about one's general outlook on life.

I'll never forget the first time I took the *Myers Briggs Personality Test* as part of the seminary admissions procedure. It was based on the psychologist Carl Jung's finding that people can be classified using two mental functions (sensing-intuition and thinking-feeling), attitude (extraversion-introversion), and a fourth dimension that helps determine the dominant function (judging-perceiving). Wait! Lighten up! We don't have to know all this in order to profit from the results of the test! Take it from me, I was nonplussed and humbled that a *computer printout* of my test results had me down cold! It knew me better than I did! And it helped me so much.

If you are working with (or *married to* or *parents of*) someone, it could be really helpful to know their *personality type*. Since we don't *choose* our personality (and because it is so much a part of us that we are not good judges of its good or bad aspects!), the more information and help we can get the better. When I was a member of the seminary faculty (of fourteen people), we decided to share with one another our Myers Briggs personality types. Since no one is to *blame* for her or his personality type (it just *is*), it was freeing and valuable to know that so-and-so's constant *delaying* our decision-making wasn't due to his being negative or *ornery,* he just needed more input and time for reflection than the rest of us. Someone else had an annoying tendency to *jump to conclusions*—and we could keep that in mind to guide our discussions.

Part of the beauty of knowing our (and others') personality type is learning how to live and work together more effectively and peacefully. The impatient feelings that spring up may be based more on deep differences in personality rather than a prideful unwillingness to see it someone else's way. Or what strikes a certain person as shallow or frivolous may, to the offender, be simply a more joyous way of approaching life.

But because one's personality simply *is* doesn't mean that anything goes! Those who have studied this area find that traits or characteristics can have helpful and positive aspects, but some are inclined to have a *dark* or limiting side which needs attention and compensation. My hope is that you find this whole area as intriguing as I do. Further knowledge of one's own and others' types of personality can lead to greater personal freedom and genuine spiritual growth.

I have found some resources (online—therefore, *private!*) which you might find very interesting and valuable. The Myers Briggs Personality Test may be taken free of charge so you can determine your own four characteristics—and then read the insightful descriptions. I believe you will be fascinated (as I was!). Go to the site: http://www.humanmetrics.com.

When you have taken what you want from that method, there is another site which deals with similar insights into personality according to a different classification (into nine areas) and which is also extremely interesting and helpful. The site is http://www.enneagraminstitute.com.

The Teaching Church and You

Of one thing I am quite sure. There is certainly no agreement among popes, bishops, priests, committed and faithful laity, and many others open to the Gospel and the beliefs of the Catholic Church regarding *how* the preaching of the Gospel and communicating the beliefs of the Church should be done. This may seem to be a sweeping and negative evaluation of all the above but, as often in life, there are many factors which have caused the current situation. This reflection is not to cast blame, but to try to help *you* (and me) understand where that leaves us today as Catholic Christians.

As a matter of fact, there are so many circumstances which have led to our current predicament that I am not gifted enough to present them in a logical or timely order—but let's launch into it, anyway. Jesus commissioned his apostles, "Go therefore and teach all nations" (Mt. 28:19) and said that Peter was the *rock* on which was built the visible structured community of his followers. We know this as the *Church*. From this flows the need to have a *teaching authority (service)* so that the accuracy of insights faithful to the Gospel will be shared over the centuries. When this service is communicated well in humility and truth, one would have to grant that this is a great gift to the Church's faithful, instead of their being *blown about* by ignorance, emotions, differing opinions and needs, and other distractions which human beings manage to provide so abundantly.

We are not suggesting that what is a *Pilgrim Church* (a suitable term used frequently) is now or has ever/always been perfect—in its institutional structure, in the very *words* used at a given time to express its doctrines, in its full recognition of the many gifts God has given it (e.g. sacraments, social teachings)—or even in its openness to development or change, or really listening to the insights of the faithful. We do not believe, however, in a *Deist* God who set everything up and then left us alone to our own devices. But our true belief as Catholics is in a God who has shared *freedom* with all human beings and gave us all enough room to *make mistakes*, no matter how *honest or important* we believe our conclusions to be. It is true the Holy Spirit is always present to guide us, but that does not mean that everyone (or anyone) is listening!

Let me draw (with a broad, therefore imprecise brush) a picture of what I see today. After a great deal of thought and prayer, I find I must use a method which means, unfortunately, that the reader will have to do some work—separating each of the following factors/insights/thoughts so that time can be spent evaluating its importance. May I suggest that—in my opinion, at least—each consideration is both true and also part of our quest to understand the *why* behind the *how* the *official* Church teaches.

1) Popes and bishops, as the traditional *magisterium* or *teaching authority (service)*, are both helped and hindered by the past (helped: by the ongoing tradition of the Church's teachings; hindered: by feeling unable to change what they believe or have been taught is actually true);

2) Part of our official teaching is that the *sensus fidelium* or *the lived opinion/experience of the faithful/laity* must be seriously considered by the teaching authority. In regard to some of the most controversial moral issues in our time, the opinion/practice of the Catholic laity has seldom been taken seriously—contraception to regulate/space birth or prevent infection; masturbation as *natural* and not sinful in the vast majority of cases; requiring end-of-life means to keep someone *physically alive* instead of respecting the *dying process* as having begun; rethinking and reformulating our Church teaching on human sexuality—incorporating values based on the life experience of faithful married Catholics (and also faithful single Catholics, even those with a same-gender orientation), seeing not simply the physical/biological aspects of a person (since we are also animals), but also

the spiritual, emotional, and psychological components (because we are *rational* animals!); and

3) In today's reality, we must face two (at least) very significant impediments to teaching (or learning) effectively anything regarding the Gospel or the Church. The first is the bombardment of *facts* (news, information) to which we are all regularly subjected, compounded by the excessive *busy-ness* of most people's daily lives. No time or incentive to think deeply about *religious* issues? The second obstacle, even for most Catholics, is an inadequate background both in *what is* the teaching of the Church and *what are the reasons for it.* Add to this the pervasive *secularism* of society in general (i.e., perhaps consciously unaware but living and working daily as though *there were no God).* So why spend the time and energy to listen carefully to what is irrelevant to one's life and which is frequently ridiculed by one's culture as *out of touch* or *imposed* by authority?

I am thankful, humbled, and joyful for having been given the Catholic faith. It is where I find friendship with our Father, Jesus, and the Spirit. The challenging but comforting words of the Gospel remind me who I am, and unite me with all human beings, especially those most in need. We worship and are nourished together, we hope together, we serve one another. I am part of a constantly self-discovering Church, no longer feeling obligated to kill those who will not join her or, at one period, who *required interest to loan money,* or a Church which approves of slavery, holds Inquisitions or Crusades, but finally through God's grace has rejected some of history's worst stupidities. Gender equality, deep mutual respect among those who must recognize how we are all teachers and learners at the same time, joyful and caring articulation of God's gift of human sexuality, respecting human life and the complexity of its inbuilt dynamics— more serious challenges for the Church as it continues to self-discover the fullness of the mission God gave it.

Take a deep breath. This is no simple solution. But *until the doctor comes,* as they say, we must each live our daily life in this mixed climate of grace/wisdom/faith/joy and disappointment/confusion/frustration /questioning. So did the contemporaries of Jesus.

Meanwhile, regarding *what should I do right now* about such and such? You might find assistance, as I do, by rereading the thoughts on *conscience*. (Page 13) It helps somewhat to focus the fuzzy picture which is *life*—at least, on the occasions when I must decide what to do about something.

WHAT MATTERS

Here's a story I heard a long time ago—and it summarizes "What Matters:"

"When you die and get to the pearly gates, you'll see St. Peter there, and behind him are gathered *all the poor of the world*. He turns to them and asks, 'Do any of you know this person?' And if even *one* of them does, you are in!"

I love that story because it gets right to the point—but I am chastened by it because it doesn't leave any *wiggle room*. It puts *teeth* in Jesus's second great commandment: "You shall love your neighbor as yourself". In 1 John:4:20, "If anyone says 'I love God,' yet hates his brother, he is a liar. For anyone who does not love his brother, whom he has seen, cannot love God, whom he has not seen."

"Everyone should look upon his neighbor (without any exception) as another self...lest he follow the example of the rich man who ignored Lazarus, the poor man... Today there is an inescapable duty to make ourselves the neighbor of every man, no matter who he is, and if we meet him, to come to his aid in a positive way, whether he is an aged person abandoned by all, a foreign worker despised without reason, a refugee...or a starving human being who awakens our conscience by calling to mind the words of Christ: 'As you did it to one of the least of these my brethren, you did it to me.'" (Second Vatican Council)

The Council emphasizes those crucial words of Christ *which is the only place in the entire Gospel that Jesus Himself gives us the criteria for salvation* (Matthew 25:31–46).

As human beings, many attempt to pick and choose which *acts of virtue* or *obligations of Catholics* they personally decide are a sufficient *insurance premium* so they can be sure to be *saved*. (As if God,

Who *is* Truth, can be placated or fooled by our personal construct measuring the *least* required of us to be worthy of eternal life).

But isn't it enough that we go to Church regularly, are fairly honest and truthful, love those who love us, aren't usually racist, and give from our surplus to those less fortunate? Let's just consider *regular worship* for a moment. That is truly a necessary and wonderful celebration of one's life with God—provided we are there *to be fed Jesus, body, blood, and word,* and to strengthen and support one another *so none of us ever neglects the works of mercy in our daily lives.*

Let us once again highlight (and encourage each of us to read and consider the whole passage, Mt. 25:31–48) because it is the *only place where* Jesus *tells us what is necessary for our personal salvation*:

> *"I was hungry and you gave me food,*
> *I was thirsty and you gave me drink,*
> *I was a stranger and you welcomed me,*
> *Naked and you clothed me,*
> *In prison and you came to visit me."*

> *Then the just will ask Him, "Lord, when did we see You hungry and feed You, thirsty and give You drink? When did we welcome You away from home or clothe You in your nakedness? When did we visit You when You were ill or in prison? The king will answer them: 'I assure you, as often as you did it for one of My least brothers, you did it for Me.'*

WHAT DOES HE REALLY KNOW?

Those of us above a certain age could finish this script. It's Sunday morning and Mom is heading to the car with the three youngest. "Dad, find out what's keeping Jimmy. I've been calling him for half an hour."

The father lets the screen door slam as he heads up toward the sixteen-year-old's room. "What's going on here? You're not even out of bed!"

"I'm not going, Dad."

"Of course, you're going to Mass with us. Get up!"

"I don't get anything out of it, why do I have to go?"

"As long as you're under my roof you're going to Mass, so get yourself ready, and now!"

Jimmy was motivated by a couple of Dad's subsequent threats about no TV, etc., and now they are home from Mass and the sulking Jimmy is back in his room.

"I really don't know what's gotten into him. He knows he's supposed to go to Mass."

End of scene.

The question is: What does Jimmy *really know?* As a matter of fact, during the car ride when Jimmy pressed Dad as to why this was so important, Dad had a difficult time coming up with any reason other than obedience: "Catholics go to Mass, and you're a Catholic. It's a sin to miss." Dad scores high on being conscientious but doesn't come out as well on knowledge. He didn't really *know* either why Jimmy should be at Mass.

We should look at the *two* levels of knowledge which are involved here. *Conceptual knowledge* means simply that the basic demand or bare principle has been heard and is now remembered. *Evaluative knowledge* signifies the person really understands the meaning of the *value* which the bare principle or norm is meant to convey. The goal of moral teaching and preaching is to help people deepen their understanding of the Gospel and our Church community's wisdom on how to live a full human life—to move from conceptual to evaluative knowledge. Not just *what*, but *why*.

Obedience is a necessary virtue, especially for children whose immaturity or inexperience can make evaluative knowledge very difficult to achieve in certain areas. Even Dad may be going to Mass simply out of obedience, but he and Jimmy deserve better. They owe it to themselves and to God to come to an evaluative knowledge of the place of Eucharist in their lives. It will be the crucial difference between "Catholics have to go to Mass" (conceptual knowledge plus obedience) and "We're called as members of God's family to join together in Jesus's own prayer and sacramental nourishment—in thanksgiving, celebration, unity, and support" (evaluative knowledge).

Every commandment or moral teaching tries to incarnate or make concrete a gospel value. We can't take it for granted that people have come to an evaluative knowledge of what the demand really means. *More important is that serious moral activity in the sense of personal growth in virtue can occur only after evaluative knowledge is present.* A person must not merely know *that* something is right or wrong but *why* it is so. Then childlike obedience can give way to responsible personal action when faced with good or evil. Obedience to God's plan for us is then swept up into standing right with God—seeing the truth as God sees it.

"Thomas Aquinas explains it in this fashion. To be free, a person must act of his own accord and, therefore, when he is impelled by another there is no freedom. He goes a step further and says that not only a person but a precept could take away freedom if that becomes the sole motivation. 'He who avoids evil not because it is evil, but because a precept of the Lord forbids it, is not free. On the other hand, he who avoids evil because it is evil is free.'"

Vatican II Council echoes Aquinas, "Children and young people have a right to be encouraged to weigh moral values with an upright conscience, and to embrace them by personal choice" (McNulty, *Invitation to Greatness*).

For parents, religious teachers, and preachers, the obligation is crystal clear. Merely stating the norm or command is never enough. Every person deserves a sensible, cogent, and attractive presentation of the purpose/value the norm helps us achieve. Then *what she or he really knows* is the truth which can set them free.

Doing Whatever I Want

Anyone familiar with meetings or other gatherings of people knows from experience that for any random group of twenty, there are probably at least seven or eight different opinions on any topic raised! But I've had a private poll going for many years which comes up with much greater agreement. When I'm with someone in the twelve-to fourteen-year-old age bracket, I can't resist posing the question, "What's your idea of *freedom?*" The almost knee-jerk response has been, "Doing whatever I want!" The unfortunate but not too surprising reality is that many adults echo the same wistful longing.

For the philosopher or theologian, freedom has always been seen as a good. But one needn't have great experience with human living to realize that *doing whatever I want* in every situation results in mixed blessings at best. One cannot reasonably expect universally good results from the snortings and chargings of an unbridled ego.

Freedom *is the root power of self-realization in community.* As such, freedom is always a good, and we use a different term *license* which quite adequately stands for the negative possibilities of self-destruction or stagnation.

Most normal people want *to be somebody.* For most of us, this implies nothing as grandiose as making the cover of a weekly magazine or ending up as chairman of the board. It's just that we want to be somewhat comfortable with the person in the mirror on the many mornings yet to come in life. For the most part, we try to choose the alternatives which enhance what can technically be called our self-realization. In our more reflective moments, we rightly recognize our life as a task or project to be achieved. *Freedom* is the word we use to describe the human power to achieve ourselves as persons.

At the same time, *freedom* is one of the powers which shows woman and man as made in God's image. We are never so much like God (and never as truly human) as when we are lovingly creating something new and good with our freedom—in this case, creating the fuller person each decision in life should help us become. We believe human freedom is a participation in God's freedom. Just like lighting one candle from another, however, our sharing does not diminish the fullness of God's freedom and the fullness of God's self-realization. And we truly add our personal *light* to the darkened world.

We must take our freedom more seriously. Life would be easy, though dull, if we were puppets manipulated through a preplanned script. Psychological determinists see us pretty much that way. I would be one of the first to admit we are very much influenced by the unfreeing forces of selfishness or immaturity, personal needs and wants, environment, and psychological manipulation. But whatever forms of slavery we sell ourselves into, don't we really sense at times, on the deepest level, the spark of self which reminds us that *I am the one who is living my life?*

The godlike power of freedom was given each person for his/her self-realization. We are invited to choose wisely among the goods available instead of being driven by subhuman impulses. This is where the many communities in our lives can either serve or limit our freedom. Do family and Church help us toward personal responsibility and wisdom? Do peers and fellow workers give us good example and support? Do my own town and nation provide opportunity and justice? When we are children, it seems that the only thing other people do for us is *limit* our freedom! As adults, we must understand the significance of our many communities in developing possibilities to use our freedom for personal achievement and the common good.

Because simply *doing whatever I want* could at times be destructive for my own growth or that of my neighbor, it can never be a definition of freedom. Rather, whatever enhances the self-realization of each person in the community must become someday, through wisdom and maturity, the *whatever I want* for each of us.

FIRST THINGS FIRST

One of my favorite stories about St. Paul is recounted in Acts and places the apostle in Athens (Acts 17). It is not difficult to imagine this clever missionary wracking his brain for the proper wedge to crack open those sophisticated Greeks. He had to find something to attract their attention and get a hearing. His eyes fell on their altar *to an unknown God.*

What an opening! In an effort to keep all their religious *bases covered,* the Athenians took no chances of offending even an unknown God! Paul would use this to identify Him as the Father of Jesus Christ, and the process of evangelization had begun once again.

Of particular interest to us is the fact that Paul started by preaching the Good News—the Christ and His resurrection; new life for a new people of God. He opened to them the meaning of their lives, the proper source and fulfillment of their hopes, the invitation to live as sons and daughters of a loving Father.

He did not begin by preaching morality.

What a strange thing for a moral theologian to emphasize. If such is true, one might think we'd seek to play it down. No, there is a place and necessity for the moral life—Gospel values in practice— but it is never properly the *first* place in time. Paul avoided that trap into which we continually fall, even with twenty centuries of experience behind us.

St. Paul recognized that the moral life of the Christian should flow from her or his faith-commitment to Christ. So he preached Christ Jesus as the source of meaning and truth. Paul didn't see how anyone could be seized by that reality and not see its implications for a daily life of loving response to God and neighbor. Evangelize the people, sow the seeds for conversion, and then the Spirit of God would guide them on the straight path. For Paul, the only ground for a moral life is a lively faith. Upon securing a base for the faith to grow, the apostle would move on to another place which had not yet heard the Good News.

But what about the many moral teachings found in Paul's letters? There is certainly no attempt at a systematized moral theology, but Paul seemed sadly to recognize that the nascent and weak faith of the infant churches had permitted inconsistencies in the moral sphere. What's this about the rich Christians at Corinth sharing Eucharist with their poorer brethren but not giving of their abundant food afterwards (1 Cor. 11)? What about sexual abuses (1 Cor. 6)? So he fired off a letter to set things right. But notice how he situates the argument.

The wealthy Corinthians are warned that they don't really understand Eucharist, that *their faith needs development.* The fornicators forget their bodies are temples of the Holy Spirit—*their faith needs development.* And we could go on and on with examples. The valid Christian moral response is founded in and makes sense because of one's faith-commitment. I would suggest that we are living in a time that Rome, and many of the bishops, priests, and well-meaning laity are replacing faith development with moralizing: that to be a true Catholic today is to be on fire against people's moral failings (in areas of respecting human life, sexuality, relationships), rather than being on fire with God and the love that includes, welcomes, supports, and forgives.

First, we are usually willing to equate nominal Catholicism with faith, at least in practice. Yet Word and sacraments shorn of continuing formation do not usually produce a truly Christian believer. How many people in our parishes, even in the pews on Sunday, need evangelization—even conversion—before moral insights begin to make sense in a way that attracts and frees? So often, after a deep experience of God (maybe an encounter, prayer group, *lock in*), the very people, young or old, who thought the Church archaic in its moral norms begin to see for themselves the beauty of justice, worship, respect for others, or forgiveness. Yet instead of following Paul by finding ways to make appealing the truth of God's unconditional love and saving presence, leaders chafe or rail at the results of what is a premature and ineffective moralizing which then becomes a new legalism.

Second, too many leaders and laity equate religion and morality. I fear that for many, the Catholic faith has been reduced to living a specific code of morality. Observance of moral norms should *flow from faith and the meaning of life,* not replace them. Through attention to the wonders of God's unconditioned love, let us bring some hope to spiritually starved people. If we believe in resurrection, why do we come across as *scolds* instead of joyful, hopeful, and free to one another, let alone to the eyes of nonbelievers? The true concerns of religion are to answer people's deepest needs and give them the courage, strength, and hope to meet moral challenges. But to stress the moral challenges alone, as though this were the extent of Christ's message and the Church's purpose, is to send people on a desert journey without water.

People thirst for the Living Water. Let us call this Spirit by name and preach her Living Presence in each and every believer. The Spirit's moral guidance will make little sense to those who still have an *unknown God.*

THOU SHALT...

Somewhere along the way, morality has acquired a bad name. For those people who insist on making themselves number one in life, it's easy to see why they reject a morality which emphasizes respect and love for others. Self-serving is marketed under many different labels—"I've grown up" "No one has a right to tell me how to run my life" "I've got to be me" and so on. Some preachers say such people aren't really happy. I would suggest they probably are happy (because of sufficient distractions), but they are surely not joyful—and it's only joy that lasts because it flows from inner peace.

There's another group of people, however, about whom I'm rather concerned. Let's call them the good Christian believers who have their hearts and heads in the right places. A good percentage of these fine people are being shortchanged. Their attitude toward morality is not different enough from the scoffers mentioned above. Their goodness keeps them open to the moral wisdom of the Church community, but many have not yet seen its creative and life-giving qualities. For too many of the faithful, morality is the *bad news* you have to put up with in order to get in on the benefits of the *Good News*.

One gets the impression of a person paying an insurance premium. He certainly doesn't relish such activity, but it's the only way to keep his coverage. It's very easy to fall into the notion of a pagan god. "I don't really trust this god and unless I do certain things to keep him happy, he's going to get me!"

Does this sound far-fetched? I admit, most people aren't relating to moral demands in such a consciously negative fashion. But it happens, nonetheless. Someone starts feeling guilty that she hasn't said her prayers regularly enough and secretly hopes there's time to make up for it before God notices. A good business deal falls through, and the man fleetingly ties this failure to his lack of regular attendance at Mass. Illness strikes, and there are suddenly many promises to live a better life if God will only make it go away.

These superstitious and mechanistic attitudes toward God and moral norms strike at the very heart of faith. On the one hand, they portray a capricious and untrustworthy god who must periodically be placated. On the other hand, moral norms are treated as though they had no real value for promoting a more rewarding human life. Just obey some more rules and you've paid your premium for a while longer. It almost doesn't seem to matter which laws I obey provided they outweigh my sins. This reminds us of a very old heresy: God doesn't save me; I earn my own salvation by obeying enough rules enough of the time.

Perhaps the negative phrasing of many commandments and moral norms—"Thou shalt not..."—has contributed to the popular mentality that a moral life limits our freedom and is simply drudgery to be endured. But far from promoting unfreedom, the moral choices liberate a person from the bonds of selfishness, sin, or ignorance. These guidelines call our attention to what is known to be humanly destructive; what harms the person and the community. For every "Thou shalt not..." there is a corresponding positive invitation *to join in co-creating with the Spirit a redeemed but unfinished world.* This is a major theme of Church teaching and can be surprisingly exciting and involving.

Do not kill becomes an invitation to work that life might be respected in all its forms—the aged, disabled, the unborn, the poor, prisoners, human rights, peace, the environment. *No adultery* becomes the challenge to grow into a warm, faithful, and caring person. A Christian sexuality frees a person from the mistake of using someone instead of caring about her or him—and from being used.

I'm reminded that in the Middle Ages there was a monastery where the monks would break up their intense periods of prayer by weaving baskets out of straw. They soon had enough baskets for their needs, but they kept on basket-weaving for their recreation periods. But now they would use the next period to take apart those same baskets!

I don't think anyone, especially the young who are beginning to get a taste of life, really wants just to settle in and feel that all the adventure is gone, all the paths have been paved, all the frontiers have been explored—that life is just basket-weaving. What are we going to do to help them—and us—realize that one of the most dynamic challenges in life is to live as a committed follower of Jesus? Being a morally good person is important and creative. I can fill in the emptiness and hurt of hatred and injustice with my caring and loving. My personal strength and sense of fairness can bring healing where there is dissension and pain, truth and openness where there is suspicion or lies. *Co-creators with God of a redeemed but unfinished world.* "Thou shalt..." Now *that* is exciting.

THIS *LOVE* STUFF

As I was getting ready for Mass one Sunday a few years ago, an older gentleman of my acquaintance stormed into the sacristy, saying to anyone who would listen, "I'm sick of all this *love* stuff! That's all we ever get in sermons anymore." It had taken me many years, but I had finally learned when to be silent.

And yet he had a good point. I, too, am concerned that *love* is an overworked word. In a number of homilies I've been privileged (or condemned) to hear, it has been used as a catchall term given no precise definition. The preacher seems to assume that everyone knows what love means. St. Augustine very trustingly implied as much when he advised, "Love, and do what you will." But everyone doesn't know.

Let's flesh out St. Thomas Aquinas' definition of love: "Love is effectively willing the true good of the other." Since we're traveling in such heady company, we'll respect his philosophical method and consider the definition in parts. Let's start at the end with *the other.*

Love is properly *other-centered.* We must never deny the importance of proper *self-love,* but that term really means *self-appreciation.* One who is very insecure will not be able to concentrate his or her energies into service for others. They'll be too preoccupied with the type of impression they're making, whether they're affirmed or rejected, and so on. To be able to love others deeply, one has to be fairly well *together.* Then she or he can direct themselves to the other's needs.

The *true good* of the other. A great theologian, Karl Rahner, makes the point that Jesus obviously felt he could *command* us to love God and one another—even our enemies. Then most certainly our Lord did not confuse love with emotion. Emotions cannot be commanded, yet Christ did command that we love everyone. Whether we *like* them or not!

What God asked us to do was work for one another's true *good*. Not just plain *good* in the sense of what a person might think is good for her here and now. A child might be delighted with a shiny knife or matches, but we don't love him by encouraging such playthings. A parent's discipline can be a sign of deep love if its goal is the child's true good. We are commanded to love even an enemy or wrongdoer—at least by working and praying for their conversion or change of heart. The command of Christ never lets us *write off* anyone as hopeless or unworthy. Our commitment must not simply be to *whatever they want,* but that their true good be accomplished. We must always be *for* them.

The final phrase is *effectively willing* their true good. Even if we at times surmount the difficulty of keeping open to everyone ("Who is my neighbor?"), we can easily strike out on this last point. Consider prejudice for a moment. If I am not in a position to affect racially motivated hiring practices, then perhaps such unjust discrimination can be only an object for my prayers. But what if I own the firm? In either situation, to be a loving person means to *effect* what I can for people's true good. To be content with prayer and good wishes for those treated unjustly when I could *effectively will and accomplish* fair hiring practices is not love but self-deception.

It is obvious that not everyone can do everything for everybody. But we must realize that *love has content.* When we talk about love we must discover the specific content which fits the occasion. It's not simply a warm or nice thought. Love demands that those things which make up a person's true good must be promoted by our personal energy and commitment. Justice, truth, respect for life, fidelity, compassion, and so many other gospel values provide the content of love (Cf. 1 Cor. 13). Just imagine a world where, for one another, we all effectively worked for the true good that *was* within our limited power! The face of the earth would be renewed. That seems to be what Jesus had in mind. It's what this *love* stuff is really all about.

How to Be Kind

"Always be welcome anywhere" was offered earlier for our reflection. Here is a really helpful piece by Katy McColl (*Good Housekeeping*, July 2012). She has, for me at least, expanded my thoughts on how to be *kind*. That virtue not only makes us extremely lovable, it also fulfills Jesus's emphasis on *love your neighbor*. My approach was to print out her suggestions and put a check next to the ideas which most appeal to you and *get to it!*

*   Leave a bouquet at the hospital—the nurses will know who needs it the most;
*   Curb road rage—let other cars merge onto the highway;
*   Leave your neighbor a note or tell them how much joy you have in admiring their garden;
*   Arrange to pay anonymously for a soldier's or old person's breakfast when you see them dining alone;
*   Don't show impatience with someone ahead of you in a supermarket line;
*   Drop off combs, toothbrushes, or toothpaste at a shelter or food pantry;
*   Shower the pediatric wing of a hospital with $1 coloring books or crayons;
*   Carry someone's groceries;
*   Send a thank-you note to the brave officers at your local police station;
*   Check "Yes" to be an organ donor and tell your family;
*   Bring courtesy back in an instant: hold the door for someone, smiling at them;

* Sing an employee's praises to a manager or on a comment card;
* On trash day, wheel your neighbor's can out to the curb or back to the house;
* Leave a copy of a book you love with a note for the next reader on the train or bus;
* Relay an overheard compliment;
* Pause and give people the benefit of the doubt (in conversation or with e-mails);
* Load extra change into the vending machine to buy the next person a treat;
* Forgive someone. Repeat as necessary;
* Volunteer to read to kids at an after-school program;
* Avoid *looking for trouble;*
* Strike up a conversation with someone standing alone at a gathering or party;
* Walk a dog at your local shelter; and/or
* Ask someone sincerely what you can do to help.

The Goodness of People

The goodness of people. The goodness of people.

Could we say it enough? Do we believe it? Is it just a nice phrase? A prior reflection considered ways to be *kind*. That's how Jesus's commandment to us to "Love your neighbor as yourself" finds concrete, specific ways of being realized, put into practice—*kindness*.

Those in too many areas of the US didn't need to read a list. Life provided the *raw material*, and *the goodness of people* came through loud and clear, in thousands of examples of people generously looking out for others—family, the people next door or across the street, strangers. They had been doing it night and day for weeks and are still doing it, in spite of being without electricity, light, heat, running water, or food. If you didn't live in those areas, you might have missed the hundreds of astounding stories in daily newspapers, on the TV channels, or perhaps personally experiencing the care, the help, the thoughtfulness of others toward you since one of our severe hurricanes turned lives upside down. People whose security, lives, and homes were devastated did not *hunker down* in self-pity or despair. No matter their age or limitations they kept reaching out, hoping, and doing for one another. As Churchill once said, "If you're going through hell, keep going!" They did and they still are.

Then imagine yourself in those circumstances. They are real people, like you and me, and they are amazing without their even knowing it. With all the problems or concerns we ourselves may be facing in life, we could all use some reinforcement. *The goodness of people!*

FRAGILITY OF PHYSICAL LIFE

Sen. Robert Kennedy had just finished speaking at a major rally for his presidential run, walked offstage toward his car, and in the hotel kitchen was fatally shot by an assassin. A middle-aged banking executive had just risen from his office chair and died almost instantly from a burst aneurysm. A teenager lost control of his car on a slick road, and he and his two passengers lost their lives as it slammed into a tree. Twenty elementary school children and six of their faculty were shot to death by a mentally disturbed gunman. A man having a peaceful dinner with twelve of his close friends would be dead in less than twenty-four hours, nailed to a cross.

Physical life is fragile. We know it, yet are always caught unaware and very often, deeply shocked. We think there should be some kind of *warning;* something which lets a person get ready for it—maybe even have a chance to avoid it. If there has been a serious or terminal illness then, no matter what suffering or grief it causes, at least death has been anticipated. But no amount of *wishful thinking* should distract us from the fact that physical life is very fragile.

Since there is truly no way to predict what is for that very reason rightly called *sudden death,* as people of faith, we must prepare to deal with this sometimes tragic or *senseless* event as best we can. Does it sound overly depressing to say that *death is a part of life?* But it is. Even Christ went through death on his way to resurrection. But no matter how fragile and vulnerable *physical* life is, *everyone* continues to live as themselves forever.

On Friday, December 14, 2012, a mentally disturbed gunman killed twenty little schoolchildren and six faculty members in Newtown, Connecticut. We may never know his reasons, but *we know from God* (not from me or the Pope, but from God's very many words to us in Scripture) that God did not cause that horror. God does not deserve the blame for our abuse of freedom, our excesses, stupidity, or our poor judgments.

Where does God enter the picture? God has been there all along, intimately concerned and present to each person at every moment of their lives. If I, with my limited sense of mercy and compassion, am distraught by children's sufferings and a family's loss, what must be felt by Christ who wept at his friend Lazarus's tomb?

God is present to sweep up to himself the child who would have been shot—to make the point strongly—even if there were no God! But there is indeed a loving God who can salvage some good from what would otherwise remain as an absurd and pointless tragedy. The child, the cancer victim, the *sudden death* are with God in the fullness of life. For those who remain, God invites and urges them to the faith, hope, and trust which can bring healing and solace. God asks them to let him help them become wiser and deeper people by facing the mystery of suffering—not because God caused it, which God did not—but because in Jesus he has been there, too, and can make their personal calvary a prelude to everlasting joy. We can trust God.

From Consumer (Stops with Me) to Disciple (Giving It Forward)

Climbing up out of the pit, into the light and fresh air:

Freedom from negativity; from *destroyer to builder;*
From slave to *life running me* to the freedom of *my living my life;*
From *we never did it that way* to *let's see if this is better;*
From *a narrow routine* to *a creative pathway;*
From *a resigned, settled Catholic* to *a cool Catholic;*
From *being alone* to *walking together;*
From *constant competition* to *mutual support;*
From *putting up with* to *embracing the challenges;*
From *boredom* to *being alive;*
From *limitation* to *possibilities;*
From *policing* to *cooperating;*
From *burdened* to *ease;*
From *obligation* to *opportunity;*
From *hiding* to *finding;*
From *ignorance* to *knowledge;*
From *obeying* to *participating;*
From *exclusion* to *inclusion;*
From *agitation* to *healing;*
From *nervousness* to *calm;*
From *busy-ness* to *focus;*
From *ill at ease* to *welcome;*
From *saying prayers* to *praying;*
From *sacrament* to *hug from Jesus;*
From *worship* to *closeness;*

FROM CONSUMER (STOPS WITH ME)
TO DISCIPLE (GIVING IT FORWARD)

From *parenting* to *nurturing;*
From *working* to *building;*
From *acquaintances* to *friends;*
From *hearers* to *listeners;*
From *closed* to *open;*
From *pretending* to *being;*
From *working for God* to *working with God;*
From *pardoned* to *forgiven;*
From *suspicion* to *trust;*
From *fear* to *confidence;*
From *judging* to *understanding;*
From *complacency* to *readiness;*
From *dismissal* to *curiosity;*
From *ideology* to *balance;*
From *party loyalty* to *truth seeking;*
From *isolation* to *warmth;*
From *self-pity* to *aiding others;*
From *keeping rules* to *self-giving;*
From *worry* to *peace;*
From *repetition* to *vision;*
From *searching* to *finding;*
From *shouting* to *speaking;*
From *problems* to *opportunities;*
From *adequacy* to *joy;*
From *shallow* to *deep;*
From *arrogance* to *humility;*
From *judgment* to *mercy;*
From *confusion* to *clarity;*
From *self-preservation* to *self-gift;*
From *obstacles* to *challenges;*
From *god* to *God.*

A MOM'S TRIBUTE

Prepare to cry. I did—every time I read this. What a wonderful little boy—a six-year-old—who was shot to death in his classroom in Newtown, Connecticut, along with nineteen other children and six teachers. And what a wonderful mother Noah had—Veronique Pozner—who offered this moving eulogy for her son less than two weeks after his murder. Let's try to celebrate life like Noah by recapturing what we each once had more of: enthusiasm, a sense of wonder and possibilities, infectious joy, and love.

"The sky is crying, and the flags are at half-mast. It is a sad, sad day. But it is also your day, Noah, my little man. I will miss your forceful and purposeful little steps stomping through our house. I will miss your perpetual smile, the twinkle in your dark blue eyes framed by eyelashes that would be the envy of any lady in this room.

"Most of all, I will miss your visions of your future. You wanted to be a doctor, a soldier, a taco factory manager. It was your favorite food, and no doubt you wanted to ensure that the world kept producing tacos.

"You were a little boy whose life force had all the gravitational pull of a celestial body. You were light and love, mischief and pranks. You adored your family with every fiber of your six-year-old being. We are all of us elevated in our humanity by having known you—a little maverick who didn't always want to do his schoolwork or clean up his toys when practicing his ninja moves or Super Mario on the Wii seemed far more important.

"Noah, you will not pass through this way again. I can only believe that you were planted on earth to bloom in heaven. Take flight, my boy. Soar. You now have the wings you always wanted. Go to the peaceful valley that we will all one day come to know. I will join you someday. Not today. I still have lots of mommy love to give to Danielle, Michael, Sophia, and Arielle.

"Until then, your melody will linger in our hearts forever. Momma loves you, little man."

THREE LIFE-CHANGING BOOKS

I am eager to share with you three books which have had in my whole life *the most positive influence, value, and help* in my relationship to God. For me, they defined and redefined God. Wow! But I mean this very deeply. As a matter of fact, I'm a bit apprehensive that you might not take it as seriously as I would hope. We're so used to *hype*—or at least, exaggeration when someone tries to tell us something very important to them. Let me list the three books in order of importance:

1) *The Holy Bible* (both testaments);
2) *The Shack* by Wm. Paul Young (Windblown Media, Los Angeles, CA, 2007); and
3) *The Shack Revisited* by C. Baxter Kruger (FaithWords, Hachette Publ., 2012).

We all have, I'm sure, recommended books we liked to friends and others. But what they make of it matters when and in what context they *receive* the book—being true to the old adage, "Advice is not taken unless it meets a *felt need."* In other words, the wisdom of the Bible is presented so frequently that if we don't appreciate the full impact the first time we hear it, there will be many other times in our lives when our greater maturity, depth, or *felt need* might permit a greater receptivity. Such was the case for me in each subsequent reading/meditating on *The Shack (2007)*, and then joyfully exploring the theology and wonder presented in *The Shack Revisited* when it was published in 2012.

In the case of these second and third books, one might read them mainly for content, or *the story*, and miss the importance of the real message which can be life-changing. In what sense? We could so easily miss the lush and verdant forest for the isolated trees.

Each of us is intimately cared for by the Triune God—Father, Jesus, Spirit—at every moment of our existence. God is always accessible to us. We live in god. *All creation flows from God, yet remains in God. God is not distant, but* down-to-earth—*here, now, aware, personally involved, helping, caring, present and active in our everyday lives, guiding, healing, and forgiving,* loving us!

Really? Yes. But even if we've heard it a thousand times (and personally I never heard it quite this way or so clearly, compellingly, excitingly, attractively), let's give God another chance to reward us, embrace us, fill us with joy. May I assure you, as a practicing theologian with an earned doctorate in theology and in union with the teaching service of the Church, that the *stories* used in representing and presenting God are all in the mainstream of Catholic orthodoxy. Some may be unfamiliar or surprising, but they respect all the important teachings of God's revealed truths. Read, pray, rejoice.

PREGNANCY SHOULD BE CHOSEN

The urge to have sex doesn't need much encouragement. But it gets plenty.

The fundamental basis for the desire comes from the way God *designed* the human being (and lots of other creatures). It comes from our being—and makes sure that reproduction takes place. Fine. And it's one of the basic urges of humankind. It is supposed to bring great physical, psychological, and emotional pleasure—and one can assume that God has no problem with that; even delights in our procreative process. Sexuality infuses loving relationships, helps us find partners who want to share building a family, welcome children, and embrace the responsibilities that accompany this adventure.

But sexual activity for human beings can be sought for many other reasons, *general, positive, and expected*—or particular and problematic. Human hormones at puberty begin to prepare the body and spirit for sexual desire and activity. Tension seeking sexual release is normal, and that shows in the almost universal practice of masturbation. Dating and seeking a desirable partner is necessary in most cultures (and we are speaking here about what is experienced in the United States and *Western practices*). Affirming one's legitimate need and capacity to love and be loved. *Passion* can also be a virtue.

What are *more particular and less desirable* goals of sexual activity for some people? *Conquest* to show one's own popularity or desirability. *Power* or *domination* to show one's importance or influence. *Lashing out or striking back—revenge* for *real or imagined abuse*. Seeking a partner to pursue less usual *kinky* activities, perhaps to satisfy a *fetish* or pursue a personal desire. Or a hundred other desires to employ sex as a means far removed from its fundamental purpose.

Our focus today is to consider only one particular aspect of sexual activity: *the conception of a child.*

The Word of God in Scripture shows clearly that human life deserves great respect—created by God even in God's own image and likeness. It was the only suitable vehicle for God to use to identify with human creation by becoming incarnate in Jesus Christ. In light of our current scientific and philosophical knowledge, it appears that this individual human life begins at what we call *conception*—the start of pregnancy. With no further radical *outside* intervention and left to its normal development, a human child will be born in about nine months.

In light of all the above, our thesis is the goal that *every pregnancy should be chosen.*

This will demand, at least, that the woman and man having sexual intercourse know as much as possible about their own bodies and state of fertility, and the possible results of their act. None of these basic factors can be assumed or taken for granted. Imagine some of the many situations where this is problematic.

In a marital context, a couple wants sex as an expression of their love or desire, but fertility is unknown. They are convinced a pregnancy at this time would be irresponsible. The husband says he will leave if another pregnancy occurs—"No more children!" They also do not use contraception or it is ineffective.

Outside of a committed or marital relationship: Sexual intercourse may be engaged in for one of the many purposes mentioned above. Let's not impute very bad motivation to the man and/or woman. Like many things in life, we often act with inadequate knowledge or foresight, with mixed motivation—spontaneously. An unmarried couple may truly be, or think they are, in love. They are drawn to express that love in intercourse, feeling it is appropriate to their relationship. We're all capable of impetuous behavior, *hoping for the best,* passion or *being carried away,* mistakes, weakness, seeking affirmation, *fun,* or the like. *But this act can result in pregnancy—beginning a new human life. The last thing they intend or want.*

No human life is destroyed by contraception. If conception takes place, however, abortion would destroy the human life which a respon-

sible person would then assume is present. If a couple has sexual intercourse, they should assume conception is possible. If they knew they would abort an unwanted pregnancy, contraception *would have been the morally responsible choice.*

Can we begin personally to deepen our appreciation of human life so that—even pre-born, conceived, and in the womb—we will care enough, plan enough, inconvenience ourselves enough, love life enough to be sure that *every pregnancy is chosen?* Tragic mistakes can happen. As part of caring for human life, however, maybe someone would generously choose to facilitate adoption over abortion? So many couples yearn for a baby to love and raise. But, either way, no one has the right to *wrap a person in shame*—God never does.

Just a personal story. I have found abortion to be extremely sad and disheartening for many reasons. But recently I saw an ad on television which included a young infant in his crib, immensely happy and playing with all his might. He was laughing and let out a loud squeal of utter delight. For some reason, at that moment, it came to me that God wants to hear that *squeal of utter delight* from every child who is conceived, who lives. Isn't that worth everyone striving that in their lives at least, they will be sure that *every pregnancy is chosen?*

WHEN PEOPLE DISAPPOINT US

When people disappoint us... What is our *knee-jerk* (Freudian?) reaction to that phrase? How sad. How true! Inevitability? "You said it!" Intellectualizing or spiritualizing it away? Resignation? Brings me down? Betrayal?

Yet no matter how much we love someone, how deeply, how totally, how warmly, *every person* will sometime, somehow, be disappointing to us because we're all *only human.* But that is not a *put-down* because being human is great...*in God's image and likeness*, loveable and loved, intelligent and free, capable of genius, heroism, self-sacrifice—but not *perfect.*

Thesis: We live in a sharply critical age. There is very little genuine listening. There is simply hearing while simultaneously judging or reacting Perhaps it's why so many millions are drawn to television shows which parade assorted *wannabes* before them; it provides another chance to critique, to demonstrate my insights. But even when commenting on what might truly be the best in art, music, professional sports, politics, governing, preaching (!?), you name it—so many people who really know nothing about it, have neither talent nor ability for it, and have never done it themselves feel completely justified in judging severely, evaluating, and proclaiming their opinion. Why? Because it is *their opinion.*

It's sad that many of us are at times so insecure as to have to assert in every conversation, no matter with whom or about what, our opinion, our *two cents.* Not just in *disagreement* (based on?), but even by *agreeing* (with what motivation? Or shared arrogance that *we are both correct!).* Yet one will never lack for occasion to do so because no matter how exquisitely and admirably accomplished the *performer* might be, no one is perfect—so there is an occasion for criticism.

It can be most disturbing if the person who disappoints us is someone we love or care about deeply. Yet we hope that every human being is growing, always changing, and as the wise writer said, "To be perfect is to have changed often enough." Someone or everyone will be disappointed and tempted to judge when they encounter anyone who has not yet changed enough—be they my child or my parent or a public figure. But do they *stand apart* from the person, or show rather, that they are still *on their side?* What a difference.

Since the purpose of every one of these reflections is to help us more fully to exercise our *freedom*, what are the most destructive results of all the abovementioned eagerness to assert our critical and often negative opinions or judgments? 1) We could miss or not profit enough from any positive growth-affording new truths and insights—as well as appreciating this unique person who is now offering them; 2) We miss the enlightenment, challenge, and possibly the wisdom that would come into a life that was not so insecure, prematurely foreclosed, or intellectually shallow; and 3) Always looking for what we think should be there—but isn't—gets us in the habit of negative thinking and is depressive rather than engaging and enthusiastic. It limits both our openness and our compassion.

Yes, even people who love us deeply (or good friends, coworkers) could be disappointed by something they had needed or wanted *us* to be. We too have to *change often enough*—while being potential victims of the many severely critical people who might be *disappointed* in *us*. We cannot control other's minds or comments, only our own. So that something good might come from these situations, let's remember that exercising our own understanding, patience, kindness, and humility all enhance our freedom—and take another step toward helping ourselves and others *change often enough* to become what we can be.

WATCHING AND WAITING

I must admit that *7-Eleven* stores have played a strong role in my life. For those in other parts of our country and for those in other countries, may I explain that there is nothing quite like these *convenience stores*. They seem to be open all the time and have a remarkable array of the kinds of things to eat and drink that you *just need* or at least *want!* The turnover of customers is amazing, and you know that even if the parking lot looks full, you have to wait only a minute before a space opens up.

A number of years ago, as I made my purchase and was back in the car drinking my coffee, browsing through the newspaper while eating a doughnut, I noticed a dog that its owner had tied to a post outside the store. The dog was in rapt attention, looking every moment at the door, watching, and waiting for its owner to reappear. Noticing this phenomenon for years, I've never seen a dog tied outside—or more frequently, inside its owner's truck or car—which didn't fix the same intense and expectant gaze until its owner reappeared. Only then did the tail start wagging again.

Recently I was reminded of that by a similar but not at all amusing story on the TV news. This time the place was Syria inside a cave hidden in one of the hills near the fierce shelling aimed at refugees who had abandoned their homes and village trying to stay alive. The CNN correspondent was reporting the dangerous story of how three young preteen boys were waiting out of sight inside the cave opening for their mother to return. Their father had been killed before they fled and, for fear of starving, now their poor mother had ventured out looking for anything at all for them to eat. In the blackness of the cave, there was daylight only through a small opening. The TV camera panned the line of boys crouched just inside the opening, eyes unblinking and desperate, hoping beyond hope for her return. Her fate and theirs lay in the grim balance. I wept for them and prayed.

Every Holy Week, I, for one, would like to have that same focus and ability to *watch and wait*—intensely, with fresh eyes, undistracted by the ordinary and commonplace events of daily life—for the Christ who will celebrate a supper with us, ask us to watch with him in prayer, pour out his life in love for His Father and for us, and, yes, incredibly overcome death with a fuller life that knows no end. He invites us to *watch* with him as he again graciously presents it, since he knows we could not be there the first time.

Raising a Secure Child

What is the secret sauce that holds a family together? What are the ingredients that make some families effective, resilient, happy? The last few years have seen stunning breakthroughs in knowledge about how to make families work more effectively. The single most important thing you can do for your family may be the simplest of all: *develop a strong family narrative.*

At Emory University, Dr. Michael Duke's wife, Sara, a psychologist who works with children with learning disabilities, noticed something about her students. "The ones who know a lot about their families tend to do better when they face challenges," she said. She and some colleagues developed a measure called the *Do You Know* scale that asked children to answer twenty questions.

Examples included: Do you know where your grandparents grew up? Do you know where your mom and dad went to high school? Do you know where your parents met? Do you know an illness or something really terrible that happened in your family? Do you know the story of your birth?

They then compared the children's results to a battery of psychological tests the children had taken and reached an overwhelming conclusion. The more children knew about their family history the stronger the sense of control over their lives, the higher their self-esteem, and the more successfully they believed their families functioned. The *Do You Know* scale turned out to be the best single predictor of children's emotional health and happiness.

And then something unexpected happened. Two months later was September 11. The psychologists found the families they had studied had not been directly affected by the events, but all the children had experienced the same national trauma at the same time. The researchers went back and reassessed the children. "Once again," Dr. Duke said, "the ones who knew more about their families proved to be more resilient, meaning they could moderate the effects of stress." Why does knowing where your grandmother went to school help a child overcome something as minor as a skinned knee or as major as a terrorist attack? "The answers have to do with a child's being *part of a larger family,*" Dr. Duke said.

Psychologists have found that every family has a unifying narrative, and those narratives take one of three shapes. First, the *ascending* family narrative. "Son, when we came to this country, we had nothing. Our family worked. We opened a store. Your grandfather went to high school. Your father went to college. And now you."

Second is the *descending* narrative. "Sweetheart, we used to have it all. Then we lost everything."

Dr. Duke said the third one is the most healthful. It's called the *oscillating family narrative.* "Dear, let me tell you, we've had ups and downs in our family. We built a family business. Your grandfather was a pillar of the community. Your mother was on the board of the hospital. But we also had setbacks. You had an uncle who was once arrested. We had a house burn down. Your father lost a job. But no matter what happened, we always stuck together as a family." Dr. Duke said the children who have the most self-confidence have what he calls a *strong inter-generational self.* They know they belong to something bigger than themselves.

Any number of occasions work to convey this sense of history: holidays, vacations, big family get-togethers, even a ride to the mall. The hokier (even homemade *rituals*) the family's tradition the more likely it is to be passed down! These traditions or practices become part of your family.

Decades of research have shown that most happy families communicate effectively. But talking doesn't mean simply *talking through problems,* as important as that is. *Talking means telling a positive story about yourself.* When faced with a challenge, happy families, like happy people, just add a new chapter to their life story that shows them overcoming the hardship. The bottom line: if you want a happier and more secure family, create, refine, and retell the story of your family's positive moments and your ability to bounce back from the difficult ones. Your family will thrive for generations to come.

[This abridgement relies heavily on "The Stories That Bind Us," *This Life*: Bruce Feller (*New York Times*, March 17, 2013).]

It's Just Their *Temperament!*

If a priest is *of a certain age,* he remembers that in his younger years the average parishioner seldom even criticized him to his face, let alone *argued* in disagreement about something. A misplaced *nostalgia* might even make him wish that those times were still upon us—especially if he has had a particularly rough day encountering a number of people who didn't hesitate to vent their displeasure at something he said or did, or *didn't say or do.* In our better moments, however, we should be pleased that honest and open dialogue has generally become the norm—it is certainly more *Christian,* gospel-oriented, and may even serve growth and progress. No one person in a parish has all the good ideas!

When priests get together, some of the *disagreements, arguments, disputes* initiated by parishioners and which have particularly *stung* might be shared with one another. Sometimes one is *looking for sympathy* (doesn't everyone at times?) or perhaps simply running it by a colleague for their reactions/advice on how the situation was handled. You'd be surprised at how many times the evaluation of some tense encounters include the observation: "Well, that's probably just their temperament."

Since the *theme and purpose* of our mutual effort/goal in this endeavor together is to deepen our realization and increase our exercise of *Catholic freedom,* human *temperament* cannot be overlooked. It's a crucial and basic reality if we wisely take Socrates's admonition to *know yourself.*

What has become historically known as *The Four Temperaments* is not a modern-day determination or part of some *New Age* relevancy. They were originally proposed by Hippocrates about 350 years before the birth of Christ. Their realization has been part of human knowledge into modern times. No one chooses his or her temperament; it's *how we're made*. It's like a *filter* through which we see life, ourselves, events—everything. We've probably heard the phrase used for a consistently optimistic, positive, maybe even naively happy person: "She sees life through rose-colored glasses!" One can reinforce and solidify one's temperament by attitudes and actions, but it is a basic part of our life and almost always at the root of our reactions and attitudes toward everything.

The four temperaments are: 1) choleric; 2) sanguine; 3) melancholic; and 4) phlegmatic. There is not space here to discuss what is for each temperament—the characteristics, the dark side, the bright side, and special considerations in the training and treatment of each. [It is highly recommended to access on the internet a superb and fascinating treatment of each temperament: http://angelicum.net/newsroom/the-four-temperaments/.]

For example: "A *choleric* person is won over by quiet explanation of reasons and motives; whereas by harsh commands he becomes embittered, hardened, driven to strong-headed resistance. A *melancholic* person is made suspicious and reticent by a rude word or an unfriendly mien; by continuous kind treatment, on the contrary, he is made pliable, trusting, affectionate. With a *sanguine* person, we can hardly count even on his apparently serious promises; he is affable but superficial. The *phlegmatic* person has little interest in what goes on around him, has no intense passions and does not demand much of life. When he works, it is slowly but perseveringly, and remains composed, thoughtful, deliberate."

To know the temperaments of our fellow men and women helps us to understand and deal with them much better, treat them more correctly, bear with them more patiently. There are evident advantages for family and social life which can hardly be appreciated enough. It is of the greatest benefit to recognize fully one's own temperament. Only if one knows it can he judge correctly himself, his moods, his peculiarities, his past life and, *spiritually, one will know what reactions and actions are truly mine—virtues or vices.* It helps us find the truth of who we are—"and the truth will set you free" (Jn. 8:32).

NEVER FORGET

America's constant and senseless gun murders, hundreds killed in Bangladesh's illegal factory collapse (ordered into the cracked building to earn their $1.25 a day), Syria, Africa's child soldiers raped and slaughtered, multibillion-dollar worldwide trafficking of sex slaves of all ages, deaths by starvation every twenty seconds... And when will we human beings stop the incredible abuses of our freedom?

"Then I, John, saw a new heaven and a new earth... I heard a loud voice saying, 'Behold, god's dwelling is with the human race. He will dwell with them and they will be his people, and god himself will always be with them as their god. He will wipe every tear from their eyes, and there shall be no more death or mourning, wailing or pain, for the old order has passed away. Behold, I make all things new'" (Rev. 21).

Poor Church of Christ

Poor Church of Christ.
Poor Catholic Church.
No one to heal the wounds inflicted by slashing tongues of errant sons.
No one to caress the brow furrowed with dismay at the sins of your *just*.
No one to brush away the tears poured forth for those who stifle
    under *regulated* love.
It is your own children who have done your portrait with such a
    heavy brush.
Your delicate grace and youthful spirit hidden by rigid lines too harsh
    and well-defined.
Your burlap beggar's coat obscured by the rich and kingly purple cloak.
Your face which is now yellow, now black, now brown, appears so
    starkly white.
Your hands, in truth outstretched to give, are made to seem so
    grasping.
Your eyes, so filled with understanding, burn with righteous accusation.
Your lips, eager to console with hope and love, stretched tight as if
    to scold.
Our lives, our wretched features, in truth this lying portrait form.
Bleeding Church, we deform you on the rack of man's *prudence*,
    rather than accept you intact as God's *folly*.
We have bartered the joyous risk of love for the safety of conformity.
We have denied your genius to lead by our cowardly fear of the
    untried.
We have strangled your truth, attempting to confine it in the small-
    ness of our minds.
We find *lip service* a soothing alternative to the total dedication you
    deserve.

Imprisoned Church, a queen in chains, while your servants prance
to anthems of worldly praise, the dull drumming of ignorance
and jangling coin.

Poems of
Life and Death

MY AUNT HAS DIED

When I saw this house before
And entered through your welcome door,
Your hands to touch,
Our lips to brush,
My soul you'd bear
With such sweet care
And laughter ever-present there…
Now you've died.
I'm mystified.
My senses lied.
Things look the same;
A foolish game,
For all is change and what remains?
Your empty chair
Now threatens there
And makes me know how much I care.
Your picture proves that you were real,
And now the emptiness I feel
Will take much gentle time to heal.

+ + + + + + ++ + + + + + + + + + + + + + +

Winter Dawn

Seven-timed glory of the winter praise,
the wisdom of your Maker who
proves resurrection daily, never-ending
piercing light through freezing darkness...
Black, then what? Then can it be?
Then violet almost black,
then Hope, then shapes diffused
come sharper. Players on the stage
take places just in time
as footlights raise...
Is that a vein of gold between the
stolid blackest rocks of cloud?
Wearied miner's nightlong search
has brought a *strike!*
to make him wildly rich
and prove deception
by what had seemed so dark and barren...
Sun shows Son to son who has been searching, too,
and never quite remembers.
New life happens every day.

+ +

WAR

Laugh and jump about, you young and vibrant boys who jostle older
   sidewalk-sharers with your high school antics.
Drive your cars perhaps too fast, as the thrill of youth and freedom
   sends spirits racing.
Shout the drinking songs of comradeship that makes tomorrow fade
   to never.
Steal the kiss and soft embrace of that special sacred love…
Tomorrow you'll be wading in the gore and stink of putrid flesh,
Tying back the gushing blood from the stump where newfound bud-
   dy's leg once was,
Wiping from your face the splattering of grenaded comrades.
And in your times of rest, offered the young body of an unknown
   girl lonely in a land without men—and yet with too many men.
And you will scream and clench your teeth and shake your fist to
   heaven,
And heaven will echo your scream in horror of what men do to men.

TRUTH AND THE NEED FOR HUMILITY

It seems as though we Catholics will always be destined, as in the past, to be challenged by the same *liberal* or *conservative* worldviews which bedevil people's political/societal approaches to *the truth*. Take for example the church's teachings about sexual morality.

Some believe that everything the church has ever taught about sex is universal, timeless, and rooted in the very nature of things. In this view, once these moral teachings are questioned, their dogmatic foundation is weakened and everything falls apart. Any bishop who wants to remain in good graces with the Vatican is obliged to uphold these teachings in his pastoral directives.

For others, the church's moral teachings about sexuality are unreasonable, anachronistic, even hypocritical. In their view, Catholic sexual morality should adapt to important changes in contemporary culture. Such radical differences of perspective have lately turned the church into a battlefield where the opposing groups hurl insults at one another from the trenches.

To understand *dissent*, one must first understand *authority*. Authority in the church must first be based on truth. Episcopal authority is not the *source* of truth, as some would have us believe. We can *humiliate* truth when we abase it to our level and pretend to have power over it. Jesus told us that truth is a divine name ("I am the Way, and the Truth, and the Life") and to pretend to possess it, individually or collectively, is to manufacture an idol. We can no more claim to possess truth than we can claim to possess justice. And this holds for the church's pastors, as well as for their flock.

For Christians, truth is Someone who possesses *us*; Someone who reveals as much of Himself to us as we can bear. It is this self-revealing Truth who founds authority in the church. The role of the magisterium (teaching authority) is to maintain the purity of revelation by warning against aberrations, without denying or minimizing the elements of truth behind some of them. What may be true often affirms one aspect of a complex reality whose components are still not fully understood.

The church is forever *teaching* and *learning*. To deny the further elucidation of doctrine or morality is blasphemous. It is tantamount to pronouncing the church dead, no longer vivified by the Spirit, or tending to an ultimate manifestation still to come when all that has been hidden will be revealed. The reception and assimilation of God's Word by the Pilgrim Church will forever be partial and variable. It will depend partly on psychological, social, and historical circumstances. Every cultural cycle, every scientific advance can serve to deepen our understanding of revelation to illuminate one or another of its aspects. There is, however, an objective *deposit of faith* consistently elucidated through the ages to which the blood of martyrs has borne witness. The safekeeping of that deposit of faith and the upholding of the Christian moral code are confided to the church's hierarchy. The bishops are not, however, the exclusive owners of the spirit of discernment.

Historically, this gift has often been manifest in what is known as the *sensus fidelium*. This is the collective lived wisdom of faithful and practicing Christians who love God and the church and who try to live as God's people. It is precisely this inspiration which stimulates the church's growth in wisdom and grace. There is a necessary tension between the function of the hierarchy and the prophetic instinct of the people of God. That tension could and should be fruitful, but in reality, it is often bitter and sterile. It is not enough for the church's hierarchy to praise the fidelity of lay Catholics; it must also be willing to learn from them. And that requires bishops to acknowledge humbly that they don't know everything about the will of God—that it is still revealing itself to us and sometimes surprising us. The bishops, like the rest of the faithful, are still pilgrims on the way. All of us should be looking for signs ahead.

(We are heavily indebted to structure and ideas from Jerry Ryan's "Orthodoxy & Dissent," *Commonweal*, [February 8, 2013]).

BEYOND LITURGY

I'm sure it is no news to you that the revised liturgy of the Church, introduced some years ago, received a mixed welcome. No one familiar with the great variety of human temperaments can be surprised by that fact. Totally apart from any *political* religious attitudes (progressive, conservative, traditionalist, liberal), and separate as well from the fact that some people (all, no doubt, of good will and selfless intentions) delight in almost any change, and others usually abhor it unless or until considerable time proves it beneficial—any revision of liturgy is not an *easy sell.*

My goal here is simply to go *beyond liturgy* to invite reflection on some truly beautiful, compelling, community-building, and God-centered prayers and phrases which occur in the revised liturgical texts we are now asked to pray. Due to many factors present as part of any parish service or Eucharist (from poor acoustics or rushed readings to someone sneezing nearby, or our personal mood or distractions), let us pause for a moment and let the Spirit invite us into their compelling light and truth and beauty. Citations are from the new Eucharistic Prayers in the Roman Missal. (Most of these are from the final four of eight possible Eucharistic Prayers; one could encourage the priest to use these more frequently, as it is his personal choice.)

+   You have given us Jesus Christ, your Son...
    He always showed compassion for children and for the
        poor,
    for the sick and for sinners,
    and he became a neighbor to the oppressed and the afflicted.

By word and deed he announced to the world that you are
    our Father
and that you care for all your sons and daughters.

+   You are indeed Holy and to be glorified, O God, who love
the human race and who always walk with us on the journey of life.

Blessed indeed is your Son, present in our midst when
we are gathered by his love and when, as once for the disciples, so now for us, he opens the Scriptures and breaks
the bread.

+   Keep us attentive to the needs of all that, sharing their grief
and pain, their joy and hope, we may faithfully bring them
the good news of salvation, and go forward with them
along the way of your Kingdom.

+   Open our eyes to the needs of our brothers and sisters;
inspire in us words and actions to comfort those who labor
and are burdened. Make us serve them truly after the example of Christ and at his command.

And may your Church stand as a living witness to truth and
freedom, to peace and justice, that all people may be raised up to a
new hope.
    Amen.

Pope Francis Provides
Inspiration for All Faiths

[Offering a very early reflection on Pope Francis—and in a secular context (*The Washington Post*, June 6, 2013)—columnist Michael Gerson draws some inspiring conclusions for all faiths, not just for Catholics.]

"We tend to remember leaders in characteristic poses. For Pope Benedict XVI, the college professor, it was delivering a much-misunderstood lecture at the University of Regensburg, which made controversial reference to Islam. For Pope Francis, it is kneeling to wash the feet of a young Muslim woman in a prison on Holy Thursday. With due respect to Benedict's learning, Francis' symbolic act managed to more effectively communicate the essence of the Christian gospel.

"The Catholic tradition, from catacombs to cathedrals, is filled with potent symbols. There is the cross, the fish, the dove and the lamb. There is Mary's blue, the purple of penance and the red of martyr's blood. Francis excels at the symbolism of humility. He lives in a two-bedroom apartment, dresses in simple white and speaks in direct, colloquial language.

"Francis has not yet issued sweeping declarations. But his symbolism has begun seeping into substance. He seeks a simpler church, more closely identified with the poor. And he sounds like an institutional reformer. Here is the Vatican's account of one papal sermon: "When the Church wants to throw its weight around and sets up organizations, and sets up offices and becomes a bit bureaucratic, the Church loses its principal substance and runs the risk of turning itself into an NGO (nongovernmental organization). And the Church is not an NGO. *It is a love story.*"

In the context of American Catholicism, the left naturally finds this heartening. Francis is not on the verge of ordaining women priests but a reforming pope legitimizes the idea of reform. And he is also an enthusiastic critic of capitalist excess. Yet much of the American Catholic right has also welcomed the fresh air of Francis's style, while emphasizing his complete faithfulness to traditional church teaching.

Some of this good feeling is the traditional optimistic attempt of partisans to impute their own priorities to a yet unformed papacy. But there seems to be something deeper at work. The problems of the Catholic Church—from abuse scandals to corruption in the Roman Curia—seem so large that other disputes have been marginalized. If Francis's touch can stop the hemorrhage of ecclesiastical authority, both left and right seem prepared to set aside some old arguments. The result is an outbreak of patience and generosity of spirit.

Many non-Catholics have found the new pope's social teaching contradictory and confusing. Sometimes he sounds like a Latin American lefty, calling for *social justice* and criticizing *selfish profit.* Sometimes he is defiantly unmodern on matters sexual. The US media has struggled to find and apply a simple ideological label— apparently their main journalistic calling.

But this is not really Francis's problem. He holds a doctrine identical to his predecessors—one that was equally misunderstood when they taught it. Catholic social thought is not explainable in terms of left and right. Nor is it a moderate compromise between them. It starts from an entirely different premise.

Both American liberalism and conservatism put a priority on negative rights—the freedom from external restraint. For some, this means unrestricted social autonomy and choice; for others, unrestricted economic liberty. Catholic social teaching asserts that human beings have moral and social natures, and that true freedom is found in their fulfillment. Men and women are liberated by ethical behavior; their happiness is completed in family and community; and all who share a community are diminished when any are destitute and hopeless. This perspective is fundamentally at odds with moral relativism and economic libertarianism. It transcends our ideological debates and challenges all sides of them.

Pope Francis, however, is adding something new to this teaching—without which it means little. "'This guy,' says Stephen Schneck of Catholic University, 'seems to be trying to be like Jesus, the image of Jesus in the gospels.' The one who brought good tidings to the poor, bound up the brokenhearted, and proclaimed liberty to the captives.

"Whatever your view of Christianity, the example of Jesus remains one of history's most surprising constants. A man who never wrote a word, who spent three years teaching in an obscure corner of a vanished empire, still stirs the deepest longings of the human heart. When we see his image even partially reflected in another human being, it appeals beyond every political division. When we see his image even partially reflected in the church he founded, true authority returns."

"Let Your Disciple Go..."

Before he became Pope Francis, Jorge Mario Bergoglio was Archbishop of Buenos Aires. He entered into many ecumenical and interfaith dialogues. For insights into his own faith, spirituality, and very practical and pastoral sense of how to follow Jesus as His priest, we may read a book which transcribes a lengthy and fruitful dialogue with one of his close Jewish friends, Rabbi Abraham Skorka. The book is *On Heaven and Earth* (Image Books, a division of Random House, 2013).

May I offer a brief but profound insight that Pope Francis (Bergoglio) offered as the *role of a priest* in the Catholic Church:

"According to Rabbi Skorka, the *rabbi* should *lead, carry, and try to bring man closer to God.* Bergoglio explains that the *priestly* role is threefold: to be *a teacher, a leader of the people of God, and president of the liturgical assembly where prayer and worship take place.* Bergoglio describes the ideal role of a priest in a person's search for God and what sometimes happens when a priest can go overboard or be too controlling.

"The priest, in his role of teacher, teaches, proposes the truth revealed, and accompanies you. Even if he has to face failure, he is with you." Bergoglio says, "A teacher who assumes the role of making decisions for the disciple is not a good priest. He is a good dictator, an annihilator of the religious personalities of others."

"A priest dictator *weakens and holds back people in the search for God,"* Bergoglio says. A true teacher *will let his disciple go and he will walk with him in his spiritual life.*

SHADOWS OF GOD'S LOVE

When celebrating a funeral, I often include in the homily an allusion to a movie most people have seen—*The Wizard of Oz*. My goal is to help those in the congregation appreciate a little better the new experience of life into which God has invited the deceased or, if you will, an attempt to offer them a *glimpse of heaven*.

I ask if they remember that the film begins in *sepia*—a type of *brown and white*—and continues without any color until the girl, Dorothy, realizes that the tornado has dropped the house she is in back onto firm ground. When she opens the front door, all turns to vibrant glorious color—with flowers, joyful music, and lively birds singing as they fly. The *Land of Oz*, in all its beauty, life, and magnificence, offers a rich and joyful contrast which is almost *heavenly*. If we are fortunate, we all experience in our lives joys, loved ones, wonder, happiness, and, at times, find ourselves in awe of great natural beauty. But it is far from what St. Paul seems to mean by *eye has not seen, nor ear heard, what God has prepared for those who love Him.* Could one's passing into the fullness of God's embracing love and beauty be in some ways similar to going from this world of *black and white* to an experience of rapturous color, music, depth, and joy? Perhaps a *glimpse* of heaven? Worth a try.

So many of us have had such *glimpses* in other surprising and special moments filled with a deep peace, an unexpected enlightenment, happiness, a baby's smile, a rush of gratitude or freedom, sorrow suddenly turned to joy, finally knowing one is loved. These not only become high points of our day—or life—but entice us to believe that even more is *waiting in the wings*.

Is the ever-present and always interactive Spirit of God inviting us to notice even more often than we do now the *glimpses of heaven?*

(God's joyful life-giving love breaking through human endeavors and human experiences?) Jesus says he does *not leave us orphans,* and then gives us the Spirit to *teach us all things.* But our learning involves more than intellect—it must embrace intuition.

Perhaps a word more appropriate than *glimpses* is *shadows.* Every person and every experience, in addition to what we simply *see,* has its own *shadow* behind it—the fuller, richer reality containing underlying values, circumstances, virtues. When we see the shadow, we sometimes look to *fill in the blanks*—search for the truth of who this person is and why they do this, what are for them the bases or deeper implications of this experience. We intuit beyond what we see or hear with eye or ear, and can quickly leap beyond to understand and embrace the goodness, the value, the deeper sense.

Today, for me, some shadows caught my eye—in just one interesting television broadcast: an endurance swimmer accomplished her goal. I was happy for her, but the *shadow* created led me to reflect on her total joy, the culmination of her dedicated practice, her sense of well-being surrounded by affirming and enthusiastic people, what a talented athlete could do, and more. An historical segment on the great Portuguese explorers who found new worlds across the oceans brought a *shadow* to be explored with wonder at their talent, their courage, the price they paid, human teamwork, the embraced possibilities leading to discovery, all who were enriched by their finds. Reporting on a young couple whose very young daughter would live because a scientist and a doctor found a new way to employ stem cells for healing. The *shadow* let me revel in the wonder of human intelligence, so many shared hours of trial and error, and eventual success—people caring, sacrificing, hoping, praying, joyful in the end result.

And that was only one TV experience. Try reading in *Newsday* the *In Memoriam* notices on the obituary page where a notice of the person—and the sentiments of those who loved them and are still alive—is a wonderful tribute to the effect of their lives and goodness over the many years since their death. Deep love, trust that they are still alive in God, thanks for their lives with us—explore the *shadow.*

See behind the dedicated service of those who assist others in need—nearby or across the world. A news photo of one of the armed forces who has made the ultimate sacrifice. Intuit the sorrow and hope of the family left behind—and the self-giving heroism of the one who died. These are all fellow human beings who have more to give us than simple *facts*.

Every person, every life, every event has a *shadow* behind it that we can explore and appreciate. Take a moment to let intuition take us beyond the *event* or *fact*. Exploring the shadow usually brings wisdom, deep gratitude, and lets the Spirit show us more *parts* of heaven.

Plain Old Wisdom Sayings

Someone has collected these simple sometimes humorous observations which point to wisdom. There's no way one could begin to remember all of them, but why not consider each for a moment and then find *one or two* which I sense could help *me* in light of my unique personality and attitudes:

* Prayer is not a *spare wheel* that you pull out when in trouble, but it's a *steering wheel* that can direct the right path throughout my life.
* When God solves your problems, you have faith in God's abilities. When God doesn't solve your problems, God has faith in *your* abilities. (Think about it.)
* All things in life are temporary. If going well, really enjoy it; they will not last forever. If going wrong, don't worry—they can't last long, either.
* Friendship is like a *book*—it takes a few seconds to burn, but it takes years to write. (Be sure to keep writing!)
* A car's windshield is so large; the rear-view mirror is so small. This reminds us that our *past* is not as important as our *future*. So look ahead and move on. (And the past can't be changed, anyway!)
* Often when we lose hope and think this is the end, *God* smiles from above and says, "Relax, sweetheart, it's just a bend, not the end."
* A blind person asked St. Anthony, "Can there be anything worse than losing one's eyesight?" He replied, "Yes, losing your *vision*."

*   When you pray for others, God listens to you and blesses them. Sometimes when you are safe and happy, remember that it's probably because someone has prayed for you.
*   *Worrying* does not take away tomorrow's troubles—it takes away today's *peace*.

Again, I'd like to share what is one of my favorite spiritual insights—from Meister Eckhart who was a holy Dominican mystic of the fourteenth century. He said if you could say only one prayer, make it *"Thank you."* Maybe it will resonate for you as it does for me.

GOD'S PATIENCE

Wouldn't it be wonderful if everyone on earth—maybe even just all the followers of Christ—lived every gospel value and teaching of Jesus perfectly and enthusiastically? The beauty and wisdom of those goals have been written and prayed about over the centuries—and shown by example in the lives of countless marvelous people. But the fullness of God's kingdom hasn't yet been achieved by even God's most committed followers. Let's make a strong case here for reality—*living in the present moment* as though, really, there were any other choice.

Then why are we so often surrounded by people who live in the *past*, not realizing the devastating effects of today's radical confusion caused by familial and societal breakdowns; the lack of conditions for the transmission of faith and moral wisdom in many cultures (so we can no longer presume a common background or goals with a common moral language); the fact that many civil and religious authorities have eroded their own contributions through paternalism, denial of problems, sin, or criminality, unwillingness for honest dialogue; our own Church insufficiently acknowledging our traditional teaching on *invincible ignorance* and its devastating implications for people who are so *blocked* they not only can't hear the answer we might offer, they don't even recognize there is a valid question. We must begin to face the unique problems of the present and its new challenges.

The moral message of living as followers of Jesus—the One who met each woman and man as they were at that moment—is compromised as well by those who insist on living in the *future*. By this I mean those people—no doubt very good and who are perhaps making serious sacrifices to preserve their own moral rightness—who make demands on others as though the kingdom of God is already present *in its fullness*. Their harsh judgment of sinners and their frustration at people's incompleteness are an implicit denial of our Catholic belief that conversion is *continuous*—not just once and perfectly so.

Ah, the patience of God. Those who demand perfection now in every person, in every lifestyle, full personal integration, the practice of every virtue (at least those which the one judging values the most!) are like those in Scripture who ask the Master, "Do you want us to go and weed out [your garden]?" But the God who believes not merely in *second chances* but in seventy-times-seven chances replied, "Let them both [bad and good] grow till the harvest" (Mt. 13:28–29). Even in our praiseworthy hope that everyone would always do only the good, we dare not be less patient than our Father "who causes the rain to fall on the just and unjust alike" (Mt. 5:45). Jesus's attitude was *inclusive* of people, leading to growth in a kingdom *not yet,* and was harsh only toward the hypocrisy of religious people "who tie up heavy burdens and lay them on men's shoulders but do not lift a finger to help them" (Mt. 23:4).

Let us not look around in despair at the neglect or abuse of neighbor which seems to proliferate, and then deem the cause hopeless. Even in the midst of such confusion, there is still great longing for deep and loving human relationships, at times even for respect and fairness.

It might help our perspective, however, to know that anthropologists think the human race is still in its infancy. That is another way of saying that we still have a long way to go—and on that score, I'm sure we are all in agreement. This does not eliminate personal moral responsibility but it helps us understand why the more subtle values in human living are not universally understood and accepted. Particularly in the areas of sexual integration, delayed gratification, missing the *larger picture*, the desire for power or control, substance abuse, etc., we do a grave disservice both to grace and to hope if we look at so many struggling individuals and ask, "After almost two thousand years of Christian teaching, are we still only at this point?"

But Joanne, sleeping with her boyfriend, Tom who finds he is gay and cannot live alone; Karl who is shooting drugs; and Jane poorly coping with a failed marriage and two children haven't lived for two thousand years. This is the first time through life for each of them—and there is so much they truly cannot understand, and so much for which they cannot as yet bear the burden of understanding. The question for each of us is whether we can become a more *mature* disciple of Jesus, faithful to our personal commitment to God and what God is achieving in and with us, while extending a caring and supporting hand to those who are not *there* yet?

Few people are comfortable with ambiguity; most seek black and white solutions or they may withdraw. How many Christians have the loving patience of Christ to be present at someone's every fall or backward step? Must God be the only one never to give up on a person? He heard a young Augustine's anguished half-prayer, "Give me chastity, Lord, but not yet." Rather than turn away from the self-indulgent youth, God was present to him through the years until we could all thrill to a saint's lament, "Too late have I loved Thee, O Beauty both so ancient and so fresh; yes, too late came I to love Thee."

Is it the right of you or me or any power on earth to set the timetable for another's liberation into God?

Two True Thought Stories

Two groups of battleships were on maneuvers. The weather was terrible, pea soup fog, high winds and seas. The second night was worse. The captain of one battleship stood on the bridge all night, wary of secondhand reports. He didn't want to chance the battleships of the other group colliding with them in the open seas. All night he checked on the dark sky and what could be seen.

Toward dawn, an officer on watch yelled out, "Light on the starboard side, sir!"

The captain yelled back, "Is she steady or moving?"

A pause, then a reply, "Sir, she's steady!"

"Send a message ASAP," the captain roared. "Change course 20 degrees immediately!"

The message was relayed and sent. Then back came a reply on the radio that was passed on to the captain. "Sir, they suggest you change course."

The captain was furious. He turned and yelled, "You tell them I am a captain and I'm ordering them to change course 20 degrees hard now. Don't those fools know we're on a collision course?"

The message was sent. Then the reply came back. "I'm an ensign second class, and I suggest you change course now."

The captain was near spitting and the light was fast approaching. "Damn it, you tell them I'm the captain of a battleship and they'd better obey my orders immediately!"

The message was sent. Back came a reply, "I'm a lighthouse."

The battleship turned.

If we are willing to listen, does God, through church, share truths which show us the open channel *for clear sailing in our lives—helping us avoid the destroying shoals and rocks? Doesn't that make us more free?*

His name was Fleming and he was a poor Scottish farmer. One day, while trying to make a living for his family, he heard a cry coming from a nearby bog. He dropped his tools and ran to the bog. There, mired to his waist in black muck, was a terrified boy, screaming and struggling to free himself. Farmer Fleming saved the lad from what could have been a slow and terrible death.

The next day, a fancy carriage pulled up to the Scotsman's sparse surroundings. An elegantly dressed nobleman stepped out and introduced himself as the father of the boy Farmer Fleming had saved. "I want to repay you," said the nobleman. "You saved my son's life!"

"No, I can't accept payment for what I did," the Scottish farmer replied, waving away the offer. At that moment, the farmer's own son came to the door of the family hovel.

"Is that your son?" the nobleman asked.

"Yes," the farmer replied proudly.

"I'll make you a deal. Let me provide for him the same level of education my own son will enjoy. If the lad is anything like his father, he'll no doubt grow to be a man we both will be proud of." And that he did.

Farmer Fleming's son attended the very best schools and in time graduated from St. Mary's Hospital Medical School in London. He went on to become known throughout the world as the noted Sir Arthur Fleming, the discoverer of penicillin.

Years afterward, the same nobleman's son who was saved from the bog was stricken with pneumonia. What saved his life this time? Penicillin. The name of the nobleman? Lord Randolph Churchill. His son's name? Sir Winston Churchill.

Isn't it amazing how things done out of just caring or doing the right thing will come back to make you proud, grateful. We are all linked together in God.

A Right to Be Joyful?

Does each one of us have *a right to be joyful? Yes!* Next question.

Just kidding (about *next question*)! But regarding our right to be joyful? This is an *absolute right*, and it's nothing to joke about. Yet every Christmas season, we priests hear a number of concerned and honest parishioners share that, for various reasons, they *can't seem to get in the 'Christmas spirit.'* But what about our absolute right to *joy?*

This is not just semantics, but we really must distinguish between *joyful* and *happy* (and maybe recognize even the different levels of *joy* itself). [Let's remember, our mutual goal here is to become as free as God wants us to be—and sometimes that can take a little *work*—and reflection.]

Happiness can come and go, even too quickly at times. Joy *should be with us always*, and not subject to the *comings and goings* of our life: changing circumstances, needs or wants, moods, the state of our own, or our loved ones health or success, our personal losses, hopes, and fears, tragedies, or disappointments. Christ was *joyful* even on the cross; but no one is *happy* when she is suffering. And we should never attribute some *lack of faith* if, because of personal problems or serious disappointments, I can't get into *the Christmas spirit* or magically *forget* that sadness is at least for now a part of my life.

God loves each of us unconditionally and totally and wonderfully—but let's remember that we are living in a *redeemed but unfinished world!* There's a lot to be done by everyone everywhere before the full joy of our being loved, saved, redeemed by Jesus is overwhelmingly and not just intellectually but joyfully present.

Happiness normally results when things I want, value, and appreciate come together in a positive way. *Joy* is deeper, foundational—based on the reality and security of my loving relationship with God. God never withdraws that union and love, even when we sin. It is based on God's unconditional and unending love for me, personally and by name. Incredible—and humbling—but true. Scripture says it in hundreds of ways. When I am aware of and accept the truth of that deep and personal relationship, each of us has an absolute right to the *joy* that it brings.

The normal result of that *joy* for most people is inner peace. Perhaps a deep awareness of the strength that I can indeed endure challenges, trials, and tragedies because God himself is going through it with me at every moment. Not even my incompleteness, weakness, sin, selfishness, or laziness can wipe out that love and presence. Nothing can separate me from God and the *joy* God wants me to feel at the heart of my being.

People differ so much from one another. Some might feel a *warmth or enthusiasm* from this joy; others cannot either because of their personal temperament or lack of having experienced it due to inadequacies in their family or personal history. They still have the right to this joy, but its gift can be diminished by a feeling of unworthiness or—as with so many truths related to God and me—"It seems too good to be true" or "I don't deserve this." God still wants each of us to come to know that, in one sense, it is indeed *too good*— undeserved and humbling—but it really is totally true! If our sadness comes from the terrible things we hear on the news that are happening to others, we must *trust God* who also loves them infinitely more than we do.

So could we say that, in a surprising but real sense, we should just *relax?* Take some moments and a couple of deep breaths to look underneath any *unhappiness* (though it may be at this time a terrible burden). Remember that there is always in my life *joy*—whispering, aflame, and waiting for me to let it burst forth and envelope me, as God personally soothes my pain or anxiety. "I can make it; this too shall pass." A key part of my reality is God's continuing assurance that *I have a right to* joy.

BREAK OUT OF YOUR CATEGORIES

For me, many decades of ministry have come and gone but—through challenging, sublimely rewarding, or very difficult times—the deep and overwhelming feeling of being *free* has never diminished. I have come to know, however, that not every Catholic, let alone every person, lives their lives conscious of the *personal freedom* that God wants every moment for each of us. These reflections I offer as an *urgent gift*—gift because this clear and direct spiritual path has been so helpful to me, *urgent* because I'm convinced that we are living in a time when so many of the usual *categories* ordering our lives seem to be failing.

Without asking for it, we are from our earliest days put in categories. We are kids, students, girls, boys, young women or men, husbands, wives, mothers, fathers, parents, Protestants, Muslims, Jews, Catholics, Americans, Germans, Hispanic, Republicans, Democrats, employees, plumbers, clerks, bankers, teachers, and so on.

We get used to being *just another one of...*whatever categories apply. This is the first threat to our uniqueness. We learn, of necessity, how to fit into each of our categories so as to succeed. This is not of itself a bad thing; it helps us acceptably find our way. The *upside* is when we grasp and assume the good, life-giving, or maturing qualities of the category.

American: freedom-loving, enjoy and respect my own rights and others'; many good possibilities, etc.

Catholic: the revelation of God's love, wisdom, and caring in Jesus Christ; a unified community of believers, etc.

Wives: creative, life-giving, wise, caring, etc.

Bankers: guardians of our economic wealth; supportively funding new possibilities, etc.

The *downside* of belonging to so many of the categories in which we find ourselves seems in our day, however, to be dragging us down, destructively preoccupying our thoughts, creating anxiety and even anger. For years, I and more learned others have discerned what might be called a *low-grade anger* which is frequently lurking just below the surface of most people's daily lives. What would rightly be seen as a minor event *scratches the surface of our lives* and provokes a cosmic reaction. The other guy's driving gets me cursing and gesturing my displeasure—interrupting an otherwise pleasantly normal conversation. On the evening news, an extremely partisan political comment leads to frustration, anger, and upset—just the mood for a pleasant dinner together! "Where's the remote? The thing is never where it should be!" And let's not even talk about the too frequent lack of patience with spouse, kids, or my other *loved ones.*

Those unsettling personal moments are nothing compared to the disappointment or disillusionment some have with the larger categories we inhabit.

American: government and politicians are evil, no-good, and can't be trusted.

Catholic: the Pope/bishops are out of touch but want to tell us what to do; all priests are child-abusers; I don't need to go to church to pray to God.

Professionals: they just want our money and don't know what they're doing, etc.

Someone could be thinking at this point, "Granted, but my father or uncle or aunt used to talk that way, so there's nothing really new." May I suggest that perhaps they too didn't live each moment conscious of their personal God-given freedom and worth? Wonderful people, no doubt, but defined and limited by the good *and bad* of the *categories* they lived in.

More importantly, in recent decades there has been a quantum leap in dissatisfaction with the *categories*, rules, institutions, authorities, and structures of our lives. Some may be due to a former naïveté that they were better than they truly were, and now experience has made us more critical. Maybe some categories or structures truly were better then. Maybe they were always worse than we thought.

To offer an image: *we must stay* on top *of our lives.* Instead, so often we do not feel *above* the fray, but driven this way or that and victimized by our and others' weaknesses, problems, obligations, limitations, motives, stupidity, disappointments, hopes, fears, embarrassments, insecurity, duplicity, pretense, etc. We permit ourselves to be pummeled and beaten down by what we might call all these *bullies.* If we are pushed down low by life, we will never be free. True, life is not neat; life is not a picnic—and it is never completely in my control. But I can stand tall and *live my life,* not let my life live me!

+ *First Principle:* Beware of being created and determined by the categories or structures in which you live. There is a free person given life and accompanied every moment by God, and it is *you.*

When we speak about a free person, *it raises another most important reality. Each of us is responsible for her or his own actions.* Whatever action I do (or don't do, if I should do it), the act, words, omissions are *mine.* Adults must never attribute their actions to bad influences of mother, father, spouse, teacher, buddy, etc. My actions are mine. Your actions are yours. Everyone must *grow up* and accept that fact. Further, spiritually, morally, and psychologically, you or I are formed to be *who we really are by our actions.* That's what freedom really means—we make our own lives. When we live with this awareness and accept it *warts and all,* we should feel a deep sense of well-being and joy because we are *alive,* our own person, somebody!

+ *Second Principle:* Each of us is responsible for his or her own actions.

So at this point, I am in charge of living my life; aware that I am a free person who takes responsibility for her or his own actions. I am consistently (not obsessively) aware of trying to free myself from any destructive influences of my categories—and other negative forces or people, as well as my own unresolved limitations. I am trying to keep on top of my life, above the fray. I am attentive but *never worried,* since worry accomplishes nothing but waste of time and energy on something that may never happen. Rejoice! This is how life is to be lived, so enjoy it! God is always present, healing, and incredibly more patient with us than we are with ourselves. Breathe easily—omit the drama!

Generously embracing the third and final principle can and should change your life. Amazingly, it will also put into concrete practice God's two great commandments and all God's advice: "Love God with all your heart, soul and mind" and "Love your neighbor as yourself." In addition, it will make you the most loved and admired person you can imagine. You will always be welcome anywhere.

Dictionaries describe *kind* as "caring, helpful, sympathetic." The word *love* has become overused in our society ("I *love* my Buick!"). Everyone knows what *kind* and *kindness* mean. Have your car break down on a snowy evening with no one around, except the *kind* stranger who stops to help you—and you know exactly what *kind* means! Or the person who offers to give you a hand with something that isn't fun. Or the one who caringly notices *you look tired.* Or the buddy who listens to your problems but doesn't judge.

Spirituality and theology have always said that *love* includes all the other virtues. Anyone taking responsibility for their actions is attentive to the demands of justice, truth, compassion, etc. The Book of Wisdom says about God: "You taught your people…that those who are just must be kind" (Wisdom 12:19). This is not a *weak* virtue but requires attention and strength. We are speaking here of a conscious commitment that *always and everywhere, I will be kind.* When you get time, reflect and imagine what it will require to be sincerely and appropriately *kind* to each of the following: spouse (at every age), fellow worker, my parents, my child, teacher or fellow parents at school, repairman, store clerk, another driver, friends, relatives, person on line at the market, a stranger. What a sense of well-being—and a new appreciation of others—such love will bring us. It's not easy even to try to be kind all the time, and to everyone—*caring, helpful, and sympathetic.* But what a marvelous person you'll be, inside and out!

+ *Third Principle:* Always and everywhere, I will be kind.

We have looked at three very significant areas for living a more happy life. Each of us is a *free* person, given life, and accompanied every moment by God who sees our lives through our eyes and hears with our ears. We are never lonely; we are always understood. Part of enjoying and putting our freedom into practice is to take responsibility for our actions. Then we will know at the end of each day that we have not lied, bullied, or cheated our way into presenting a *phony self* who, if we are not very honest, even I might start to believe is the real me.

Trying to be *kind,* always and everywhere, takes life seriously and joyfully. Every challenge, problem, and relationship with God and with everyone else can be faced more peacefully with kindness. *Caring, helpful, and sympathetic* describes the best Christian—indeed, the best person.

COULD CATHOLIC LEADERS PLEASE LISTEN TO FRANCIS?

Pope Francis is winning hearts and minds around the world for his emphasis on mercy, personal simplicity, and vision for a church that is *bruised, hurting, and dirty because it has been out on the streets.* He rejects culture war Christianity and aloof moralizing from the safety of the sanctuary. He warns that a fixation on *small-minded rules* can stand in the way of ministering to those on the margins. A look at a few recent headlines shows that some Catholic leaders never got the memo from Pope Francis or tossed it in the trash.

A patient who suffered a heart attack at a Washington hospital recently told the *Washington Post* that a Catholic chaplain denied him last rights because he was gay.

Earlier this year, a Catholic middle school in Montana fired an unmarried teacher after she became pregnant. The superintendent of Catholic schools for the diocese defended the decision with a cold legalism that would have made proud those letter of the law Pharisees Jesus called to task.

Nothing sends a better *pro-life* message than kicking a vulnerable pregnant woman into unemployment, right? The Catholic superintendent must have missed that part in Pope Francis's groundbreaking interview with a Jesuit journal where he said, "If the Christian is a restorationist, a legalist, if he wants everything clear and safe, then he will find nothing... Those who today always look for disciplinarian solutions, those who long for an exaggerated doctrinal *security*, those who stubbornly try to recover a past that no longer exists—they have a static and inward-directed view of things. In this way, faith becomes an ideology among other ideologies."

A Catholic priest in Missouri called a woman about to attend her mother's funeral and told her he would not give her Communion at the Mass because she was in a same-sex relationship. The parishioner had served as a lector, cantor, and choir singer at the church for more than a decade. (A lesbian in the Archdiocese of Washington experienced the same treatment in 2012.)

Pope Francis?

"The Eucharist, although it is the fullness of sacramental life, is not a prize for the perfect but a powerful medicine and nourishment for the weak," he said in his apostolic exhortation, *The Joy of the Gospel.* In fact, the pope's defining metaphor has been the need for the church to act like a *field hospital after battle,* as Francis describes it in vivid terms. "It is useless to ask a seriously injured person if he has high cholesterol and about the level of his blood sugar! You have to heal his wounds."

When the Boy Scouts of America announced it would drop the ban prohibiting openly gay youth, a priest in Northern Virginia swiftly kicked out his church's Boy Scout troop. "No more compromising with the devil," the priest thundered, as he denounced *perverted relationships.*

Paging the Holy Father.

"If someone is gay and he searches for the Lord and has good will, who am I to judge?" he told reporters on the papal plane after World Youth Day in Brazil. In a lengthy interview with the Jesuit priest and editor, Antonio Spadaro, Pope Francis offers a lesson in humanity to clergy and other religious figures who reduce faith to ideology and rigid doctrine. "A person once asked me in a provocative manner if I approved of homosexuality," the pope said. "I replied with another question. Tell me: when God looks at a gay person, does he endorse the existence of this person with love or reject and condemn this person? We must always consider the person."

And then there is Archbishop John Myers of Newark, a man who wants to retire in style. The archbishop's nearly 5,000-square-foot vacation home is apparently not cushy enough for his tastes. The Star-Ledger of Newark reports that a major new addition will include an indoor pool, three fireplaces, and an elevator. The half-million-dollar tab will be picked up by the archdiocese.

I'm afraid we're going to have to call on that Argentine making trouble at the Vatican once again.

Pastors should be "close to the people…animated by inner poverty, the freedom of the Lord and also by outward simplicity and austerity of life," Pope Francis said in a speech to papal nuncios, whose job includes nominating bishops. Bishops should not have, he insists, "the psychology of princes."

Unchristian behavior on the part of Christians is as old as Christianity itself. Jesus had to remind the Pharisees again and again that their prideful defense of the letter of the law led them to defile the law's spirit of justice, love, and compassion.

Pope Francis has brought an unexpected season of renewal and hope for the Catholic Church not because he is a liberal or a conservative. He is inspiring so many because he acts like how a Christian should act. Not a bad starting point for Catholic clergy and anyone else who tries to follow in the footsteps of Christ.

(Our thanks to John Gehring, a former director for media relations at the U.S. Conference of Catholic Bishops. [March 2014, *NCR Today*].)

MERTON—A DETECTIVE STORY

Thomas Merton, born on January 31, 1915, eventually became a Trappist monk at the Abbey of Gethsemane in Kentucky—and was a *spiritual giant* who influenced countless thousands of people in their search for God and for the meaning of their lives. He was a personal *hero* of mine, and I am one of the many beneficiaries of his copious writings and tapes on contemplation, spirituality, peace, and war (as the monastic contemplative life did not keep him from reflecting on some very pressing and timely challenges to a Christian response to political and armed conflicts, especially in the fifties and sixties).

This dedicated monk hardly ever left the cloistered monastery in Kentucky and its commitment to silence. But he died on December 10, 1968 of accidental electrocution near Bangkok, Thailand.

Merton had requested a rare permission to respond to the invitation of Asian monastics to share his thoughts with them at a significant meeting to be held at a Red Cross conference center at Samut Prakan, thirty kilometers north of Bangkok. He had presented his paper that morning and had returned to his room in one of the cottages to shower and rest. He died immediately after an accidental shock from a large electric fan he turned on near his bed.

From the day the world received the tragic and unexpected news, I've always been moved to reflection on the fragility of human life—no difference in how valued and lauded was the victim.

When the opportunity arose in 1985 for a priest friend and me to plan a visit to Thailand (actually to hike for a week or so in the northern jungle area known as the *Golden Triangle* where Laos, Burma, and Thailand meet), I was determined to follow that adventure with a *pilgrimage* to pray at the place where Merton died. In keeping with the common Asian culture of not drawing attention to tragic or embarrassing events (especially of worldwide interest), after the conference was over the place was never used again and pretty much never discussed at all. *Nothing happened* was the attitude.

Fortunately, Dom Bede Griffiths, a noted Benedictine monk, was also at the conference and later wrote some details of that day in one of his books. I found it and discovered the *timeline* and a description of the cottage and the room in which Merton was staying. To spare you the details, through considerable inquiries and use of maps and translators, we hired a taxi to drive us the eighteen miles to where the conference center had been. Finally, we came upon an overgrown and almost abandoned group of small cottages—with one caretaker who knew no English. Somehow, we managed to get his permission to wander through the area and take a look at where, unknown by him, a wonderful spiritual conference of monks (Buddhists have them, too!) had taken place in 1968. The doors to the cottages were not locked, though no one lived in any of them nor did they seem in regular use.

The first two cottages did not match Bede Griffith's description of a partition-type wall which was about twelve feet long and ceiling high, but oddly open about two feet from the floor. This was the room Merton was assigned. We found it in the third cottage and opened the door to find a bedroom about twelve by sixteen feet, with a single bed and mattress in the far right corner and a tall metal electric fan up near the bed! He had noted that Merton hit his head and bled when he fell by the fan after the shock. The floor was terrazzo but no sign of anything unusual. Apparently someone had moved the bed to cover the rather large blood stain because, when I moved it away, our quest was completed. We were awestruck and humbled.

After about a half hour of silence and deep prayer—grateful for the gift to the world of Thomas Merton—and joyful that our pilgrimage had been rewarded so wonderfully, we returned to the taxi which had been waiting at the entrance to the compound. For us, it is even a few decades later as profound and real as though it were yesterday. And we still profit greatly from his wisdom and holiness. May he be with God forever.

EASTER AND *THE* *THING*
WITH *FEATHERS*

God's Promises: You are my son/daughter, I give you life, I will never stop loving you—and I have never stopped loving you, no matter what you did or ever will do.

Hope—*based on the fact that God is always true to his promises.*

The great poet Emily Dickenson wrote that *hope is the thing with feathers.* If we carry that through, then hope is like a bird: you hear it, then you don't hear its song; you see it, then it flies somewhere and you don't see it. But unlike a bird, hope never really flies away—it is always near to us, even when we don't realize it. [Scripture images the Spirit as a bird.] The three important holy days of our faith—we live this Easter preparation with hope. If we took them as merely *historical* or *playlike reenactments*, we have missed their truth, their being the source of our hope.

Holy Thursday—Jesus, in heightened awareness of what he wants to do before being arrested, gives us his very self as Eucharist; his body and blood, his very being by which we become *one with him,* fed, nourished, and *one with one another* because we are all sisters and brothers, united—actually *one body*. Christ's body. Was the bird sitting in the open window space? Hope was present at the Last Supper. Did it fly near Judas when he went out to meet the enemies, never giving up that he might embrace hope before it was too late? Was the bird sitting in a tree in the Garden? Of course. And it went with Jesus all through the arrest, questioning, beatings, mockery, sen-

150

tencing to death. It was always present, as it was with us on Holy Thursday and the silence of the vigil that night.

Good Friday—If one looked very carefully, not focused solely on him who was carrying the cross, one could see the bird darting in and out of the crowd. Hope was always accompanying him. God in Jesus wanted us to know that he would make sure hope was always present at every moment in our lives—as he lived through anything and everything terrible and painful that any one of us might sometime endure: rejection, bullying, mockery, hatred, beatings, intense pain searing body and spirit, desertion by loved ones, loss, aloneness, wondering where God was and did God care, did anyone care? Hope helped him through every moment, through it all (God was true to his promises), even the nails through his body, the pain, the suffocation, the dying. Jesus went through everything that any one of us might ever experience when this life slips away. Three days in a tomb; really dead. He knew that we had to know it to believe, as everyone else did, that it was over. Yet the *thing with feathers*, the bird, hope was in the trees outside the tomb—singing? Hope always sings.

Holy Saturday/Easter—What a brilliant song, what a soaring and darting flight when the stone was rolled away. *Hope*—God is always true to his promises—Jesus lives. *We* live. You and I live. And we always will. Jesus immersed himself in suffering, not because it was attractive or good. He knew it was necessary to go through it with *hope* to show each of us that it could be done! He did it. We can do it. Though part of our lives may or may not bring terrible suffering, we will each finally enter a tomb—while *hope* waits outside for us—singing. New and endless life found Jesus, as it will find you and me. We will join him and one another in the song. *Hope* is the meaning of Easter.

EASING UP ON LEASHES

I know I'm taking a chance, but this is being written just a couple of weeks after Easter. So it's much too soon to let the *Good News* fade away—and maybe there really are still some *flowers to be smelled*. After all the excitement of Holy Week and "He is Risen!" could we just, for a change, *float along like a leaf on the river of life?* Taking us where we might not have gone, circling for a while in a still eddy, before being gently guided to a new perspective?

Today was a beautiful spring morning—clear, sunny, light breeze, refreshing. I was walking my dog (and they are perfect models of not rushing, just leisurely moving from one new *sniff* to another). For her, an unexpected delight is coming across a tuft of new grass. She so loves searching for just the right few blades to eat that I often relax the leash to let her explore without any pressure to move on. Does anyone who holds one of the many *leashes* which bind or direct us in our lives ever think to ease up at times and just let us savor the moment? Do we ever do it for one another—i.e., remove the pressure to move on to the next thing? Couldn't we do it for ourselves more often, such as this coming week so we could *savor* quietly the new enthusiasm and possibilities which Easter brings?

My dog was a *rescue*, meaning that she had been abandoned by those who should better have cared for her. After a couple of years together, I found in a shop a paw-shaped bumper sticker asking "Who rescued who?" By then it was a question offering a truth of which I wanted to be frequently reminded and has brought many a misty moment.

Yes, as accustomed as we all become to our daily lives together with family and friends—and my caring services that go with loving someone—we can easily forget that in so many ways the person *res-*

cues me, too. Maybe what we need first from Easter is *fresh eyes* to discover some of the ways those I love or work with—by their support, challenges, demands, even *quirks*—break me out of my routines or habitual responses. *Rescuing* should be mutual, since we all need it at times. And so we have a moment to recognize it when it happens, let's ease up on one another's leashes.

SAME-SEX MARRIAGE

I am an active Roman Catholic priest. I am not gay (although I'm pretty happy most of the time—and especially when, as now, I'm able to add to the discussion some thoughts which show my embrace and respect for my LGBTQ sisters and brothers). An earned doctorate in moral theology and years of studying and teaching human sexuality, combined with extensive counseling of hetero-and homosexual men and women—and a deep love of God and the Catholic Church—all make me want to be sure every one of us comes to feel the total joy of Christ's acceptance and pride in each of us who follow him.

Although in our belief marriage was from the beginning one of the seven sacraments, it took a few centuries to proclaim it as such, and some time to move beyond simply accepting the *civil contract* officiated by the *state/government* recognizing its validity. As theology, spirituality, and pastoral care developed, today's practice became the norm: requiring that an ordained minister *witness* on behalf of God and the Church the couple's exchange of vows/commitment. Then, as well as now, our belief is that the couple themselves confer the sacrament on one another.

Not only by religious groups but in society as well, marriage was always between a man and a woman. Its dual purposes were *unity* and the *procreation of children*. Due to marriage's close connection with and even *approval* of sexuality, the emphasis had always been on the procreation of children. *Unity*—not love—remained the second essential element in the marriage contract. Whether or not the couple loved each other was not part of the essence of marriage, since many marriages were *arranged* to foster political or economic unions. As ludicrous as this might seem to moderns, most found this downplaying of *love* quite acceptable.

Apart from the physical *how-to*, society knew little about sexuality—except that for anyone officially or unofficially *religious*, sex was *morally suspect* and its abuse was regarded as fairly universal, usually *sinful* and best not talked about. For the Catholic Church, it was as recently as the 1960s that the Second Vatican Council emphasized *love* (not simply unity) as the second essential element of marriage—and in theological writing, this was further humanized as a self-giving *covenant*, not simply as a less personal type of *contract*.

If we are honest, we must recognize that *sexuality* and its physical expression can be and very often still is used to show almost anything one chooses. Positively, sex can show and reinforce deeply committed love. But it can also be misused to manifest lust, domination, control, power, possession, desirability, femininity, manhood, and endlessly more. The TV and print news every day fill out that list. In many, if not most cultures, there is a uniquely strong challenge to heterosexual men in trying to understand and live with another man's homosexuality. Some cultures promote incredible insecurity that one might be perceived as *gay* and *less a man*. Until he is secure in his own sexual identity (so easily vulnerable due to many factors beyond his understanding or control), any man might resort to mocking, distancing, false bravado, fighting, and hating—all to *prove* he is not *gay*. This all contributes mightily to an *anti-gay* culture.

Same-sex attraction as a fundamental orientation of one's life is not freely chosen. Most lesbians and gay men have known this from their youth and that it was not a choice they made. They may have repressed it; they may have denied it even to themselves. Many *married* the opposite sex to *prove normality* or *become normal.* That seldom, if ever, results in fulfillment and peace. For the *straight* (heterosexual) person, it is almost impossible to comprehend that what they themselves see, fantasize, and desire sexually in the opposite sex are exactly the reactions of the homosexual person toward people of their own gender. It was not *chosen*; it just is. *Cute, hot, flirting, love at first sight, a hunk, a babe*—the same reactions and terms spring honestly from both situations.

So are gay people *perverts? Depraved? Dirty old men? Dangers to society? Deserving of baiting, or beating, or killing? Unspeakably sinful?*

Disordered? Do we perhaps have more information and experiences in our day to help us think this through? Due to more frequent *coming out* (admitting one's same-sex orientation), most people know someone who is gay that they love and know firsthand their goodness—a child, brother, sister, cousin, friend, fellow worker. As some States approved same-sex marriage, many lesbian or gay couples have come forward, attesting to their committed unions of decades or more. They have successfully lived through their trials and joys with fidelity to their exclusive and permanent commitment. And for those who care what scriptures really meant in the cultural context of those they were written by and for, did God really want anyone made in God's image and likeness to be excluded from the love of neighbor and compassion God expects from each of us and for each of us? Can someone be *unworthy of love* if God loves them? And dare someone say God doesn't?

Regarding specific biblical texts, many scripture scholars have written honestly on the extant cultural and historical factors and their significant implications. One *classic* text, for centuries considered anti-homosexual, was really condemning cultic heterosexual prostitution; another the betrayal of the greatly revered virtue of hospitality. Further yet, much of their cultural ethos must be reevaluated since they had no idea that same-sex actions might flow from an orientation not freely chosen.

For our purposes, let's just call it *same-sex* marriage. A man marries a man; a woman marries a woman. They are incapable of physically procreating their own children by what has from the beginning of the human race been considered to be the usual way. At this point, let's not jump to *new medical techniques* which will continue to develop even further but meanwhile seduce us away from a more honest and true solution. Yes, the marriage of a man and a woman— procreating children of their own flesh—is how the human race has reproduced and will probably continue to do so. Love, unity, and procreation. Genesis portrays God as recognizing that it was not good for man (or woman) *to be alone.* To nourish and safeguard this union usually requires permanence, exclusivity, and commitment (ideally, love)—both human nature and experience validate this truth. These are included in the essence of the marriage vows.

The service of the teaching Church is to find and articulate the best ways to understand and to live the fullness of Christ and the gospel values. Then each baptized follower is challenged to incorporate generously in their daily lives the truths of those teachings. The means of articulating these truths are subject both to growth in human knowledge and effective means of communication. What philosophers/theologians in the Church tradition refer to as *natural law* has often been interpreted in a way that elevates the *physical/biological elements* of human actions to the same level of respect/importance as the spiritual, rational, historic, grace-filled, and unique dignity of the whole human person. They are not the same. The physical/biological aspects must, if a conflict exists, yield to providing for the individual the space for the fullest achievement of the gospel values he or she discerns is possible for themselves at the time of their conscience decision (e.g. how they best put into practice: faith, hope, love, compassion, service, joy, life-giving, justice, truth, etc.).

The Catholic Church has taught that God provides a special *charism* (unique spiritual gift) of celibacy for someone who follows a call to ordained priesthood or consecrated life. Do we have the right to assume God grants that charism of celibacy to everyone with a same-sex orientation who is, therefore, deprived in Church teaching of any physical expression of their love, or sexuality, or committed companionship? Would this, perhaps, lay on them a burden too heavy to bear? Each person has only one life to live. Do we believe God wants us to prevent/impede their human fulfillment by denying what is for them the only path open—a same-sex commitment through which they may truly love and receive another's love?

Same-sex marriage (not sacramental *marriage), public and validated by civil authority,* is not a *dilution* or *affront* or *against God's plan* or a *temptation to heterosexuals,* unless we falsely label it as such. *We are recognizing the union* (in love, as we hope for all marriages) *of two human beings.* The Catholic Church could welcome, respect, and support this for all those of same-sex orientation. *The Church will celebrate as a sacrament the marriage of a man and a woman*—and the blessing of procreative love bringing new life into the world. Same-sex couples can show the nurturing and life-giving qualities of their love through the joy and generosity of adoption. Married same-sex couples are following the only path open to them to celebrate a permanent and exclusive commitment to another human being, including the sexual love which is normally a part of marriage—and, as such, has nothing to do with *sin*. God does not demand the impossible.

With very little creativity, this dual approach can be a *teachable moment* to exemplify the value of committed love so needed in our society. The Church, by including all who marry, extends the embrace of Jesus Christ who loves each and every one of them, rejoices in their self-gift, and, as with all his followers, invites them to respond to the Good News which Jesus has brought us. All are part of the parish faith community of Eucharistic worship asked to live out in practice the works of mercy by service to the poor and needy, and in union with their sisters and brothers, praise the God who loves them.

Spending Today with God

When you read that title, what did you think I'd say?

Expect something *mushy?* Something *pious?* Something worthwhile but not particularly *fun?* Welcome to the human race, even the *believer* part of it.

Actually, you and I have no choice whatsoever. *We have to spend today with God.* We don't have to believe it or pay any attention to it; to God's presence with us absolutely every second of the day, whether we are awake or asleep. We never have to feel that God is with us; we don't have to talk to God—or listen to God, for that matter. The simple and incontestable fact is that you and I and every person and every part or aspect of creation *always exists in God.* Everything and everyone that exists *spends today with God.*

One might think that everyone would be delighted to know that God was so totally present to each of us, always caring, even calling us by name, from the first to the last moments of our life on earth—and then for all eternity. But we let at least two possible realities interfere with what should be our security and our delight. The first one comes from our own idea of God: impersonal? distant? demanding? perfectionist? not to be trusted (what I may have heard from the most cynical or judgmental and most nit-picking of parents, teachers, friends, authority figures)? The second interference comes from: my own lack of self-worth (God wouldn't bother with a person like me); look at my (fill in the blank)—sinfulness, pride, jealousy, impatience, sexual desires, fantasies, selfishness, etc. Most of the time no one could be harder on me than myself. How could God enjoy spending time with me?

No one has put it better than the *Christian mystic,* perhaps a monk, whose insights were shared in the latter half of the fourteenth century in *The Cloud of Unknowing.* We must remember that a *mystic* is not a dreamer or magician but one who, through God's gifts, is so deeply in touch with reality that they discern the God who is at its center and stay aware of God's presence. Here is the proper response to *the second interference* above. [Since this could be life-changing, can we spend a few minutes now reading it over and over, open to the Spirit's illumination?]

> *It is neither what you are now nor what you might have been*
> *that God sees with his all merciful eyes*
> *but what you desire to be.*

Because of God's unconditional love for each one of us, *what you desire to be* is all God really cares about. Do we feel the weight lifting yet? Whenever God looks at us, walks with us, thinks of us (yes, which is *every moment*), God sees only *what we desire to be.*

Think of human friendship. (Perhaps especially if that friendship grows into marriage.) Everyone has a past—with all its immaturity, need for growth, searching for identity, sins—*nor what you might have been.* None of us would imagine that now we are perfect—even if someone loves us now they still experience our current imperfections, need for growth, even *sins.* Therefore, *it is not what you are now that* is the primary criterion which enhances and justifies even true human friendship.

If we love someone—even a friend—it is because in our dealings with them we have seen *what you desire to be.* That is what continues to attract us and in which we find it possible to *overlook* where the person doesn't measure up to the *perfection* we might wish for them. Even now, they are enough for us. (And, apparently, their believing what *I desire to be,* I am enough for them.) We are genuinely friends.

Even while God wants for us and is pleased by our human friendships and unalloyed joys with one another, God is humbly willing to walk with us every step of life as the ultimate *fallback* best friend. Why? Because God more surely than anyone else *knows what we desire to be.* We want to love and be loved, admirable, caring, seen as good and faithful and honest because we *truly desire to be*—even *holy* (if we know what it's real *freeing, down-to-earth* meaning is!). God recognizes this is who I really and deeply am. This and so much more should make it easy, comfortable, and *wonderful* to spend today with God

TOWARD THE FUTURE

Is there some *unfinished* business which, no matter how many reflections we have already shared, I might suggest that we consider? With all the wisdom and creativity applied to the world's and the Church's problems by myriad scholars as well as by regular people with profound *common sense*, a few future directions occur to me—hoping for a clearer path toward what may be the truth we are called to know and the freedom we seek.

End of Life Issues—We must not cling to physical life as though we are deeply afraid of death. Death is a part of living. Though we usually fear any *unknown*, there is One we follow, love, and believe in Who has experienced death, conquered it, and now waits for us to join Him in living forever. Live life to the fullest we are able, but when the time to die presents itself, avoid extreme means to preserve a merely *physical* existence: avoiding suicide or euthanasia, accepting means to avoid unnecessary suffering, and remembering that at the very moment that ends this phase of our time on earth, we will be welcomed with *God's kiss of life.*

The differences *which separate us—Racism, anti-Semitism, ethnic conflicts,* class, *or economic disparities, etc.* For something so prevalent—and terrible—the conflicts and separation, even hatred, caused by these differences among us are truly appalling and totally contrary to the unity of *one human family* that God desires us to be. It is so easy to be *afraid* of those who are *different from us* in any significant aspect of our lives. As understandable as these challenges may be, *they can be overcome!* What generosity, dialogue, understanding, openness, self-knowledge, and *love* will be needed in what should be our constant attention to what divides God's one family of all human beings made in God's image and likeness?

Sexuality—Where do we begin? The Church's teaching service to help us apply the *gospel values* to our daily lives should rightly encompass the following: our sexuality is one of God's true gifts to the human person. Just as with power, intelligence, free will, and many other gifts, sexuality should serve toward love, enjoyment, self-giving, and life-giving (not only for procreating children but also for people who truly love one another). Truth, never lying, helps fulfill and enhance sexual relationships. True sexuality directs us toward the other and cares for ourselves and others as the vulnerable persons we are. Actions which may result in pregnancy are highly irresponsible if they might lead to taking an innocent human life. The expressions of our sexuality, as with any gift, need to be *unwrapped*—growing continually in understanding, maturity, respect, forgiveness, and healing.

And so...

We must walk with one another, communicating the knowledge and the experience of believers who have gone before us—theirs and our successes and failures. Then our decisions must reflect our conscience in seeking the truth of which we are capable, always loving and caring about both ourselves and others. But that is *all* the Church should do—help everyone to understand well the deep meaning and the challenging practice of those values. Enough of *proclaiming absolute truths,* implying an omniscient and uncomplicated certainty—standing apart and judging rather than walking with the person as she or he struggles. Here, again, we have too often settled for proclaiming the *rules.* Simply keeping the *rules,* as we have seen for centuries, rarely accomplishes anything positive or deep. Let's live trusting that God will make us *free and holy where we are.*

EMERGING CREATION

First there was God—only God. There has always been God.

Then there was the first atom of matter—the first thing other than God.

This moment we refer to now as the *Big Bang*.

Then *time* began.

This reflection, "Emerging Creation," will be offered in light of but not limited to Catholic Christian theology and cosmology. The few lines offered above are influenced by a *religious* faith in God. Now let us move totally into the best of *secular* contemporary scientific and astrophysical findings and assumptions before we proceed any further:

"In the beginning, nearly fourteen billion years ago, all the space and all the matter and all the energy of the known universe was contained in a volume less than one-trillionth the size of the period that ends this sentence.

"Conditions were so hot; the basic forces of nature that collectively describe the universe were unified. Though still unknown how it came into existence, this sub-pinpoint-size cosmos could only expand. Rapidly. In what today we call the Big Bang...

"What we do know, and what we can assert without further hesitation, is that the universe had a beginning. The universe continues to evolve. And yes, every one of our body's atoms is traceable to the big bang and to the thermonuclear furnaces within high-mass stars that exploded more than five billion years ago" (Neil deGrasse Tyson, *Astrophysics for People in a Hurry*).

At one point, one visiting Earth "would have found a sweltering jungle planet so warm that it was almost entirely devoid of ice and snow…and a visit 700 million years ago would have seen an Earth almost entirely covered in miles-thick layers of ice… And three billion years ago, if a human space visitor took off his flight helmet, he would have had a quick death by asphyxiation since Earth, already home to life, had air but no oxygen… All these versions of Earth have one thing in common. They were all shaped profoundly by life. It was life acting through microbes that helped set off some of Earth's *snowball* phases. It was life in the form of blue-green bacteria that first gave Earth its oxygen atmosphere… The last ice age ended about 10,000 years ago, and the planet entered a long, stable period of mostly warm, mostly wet conditions. Scientists call this geologic epoch the Holocene. Our entire history of civilization fits within it. (Prof. Adam Frank, "Earth Will Survive, We May Not," *NY Times,* 6/13/18, Astrophysics, Univ. of Rochester).

****

A STORY OF EMERGING CREATION

May I propose a story that incorporates and accepts what I perceive as enough pertinent truths from the traditions, spirituality, theology, scriptures, and revelation of the Catholic Christian Church to make this thoroughly orthodox, and you may find it as satisfying and exciting as I do?

Although *matter* has existed for perhaps fourteen billion years, we believe that God created all matter as a manifestation and sharing in the overwhelming love and mercy which is God. Through the Son "all things were made, and without him, nothing was made that has been made" (Jn. 1:3). The one God is three distinct persons in a relationship of total self-giving love. The Greek Fathers describe God in a *Zorba-like* joyful and eternal dance. *Love* has been defined as "effectively willing the true good of the other." Creation, including you and me, is God's other. Creation (everything ever in existence which is not God) has been—and always will be—emerging and evolving until the end of *time* when Christ God is shown to be "all in all" (Jn. 1:3 and Col. 1:15–16). Creation manifests God who is love, and the true goodness of all creation, including ourselves who live in that love, and who can and should share that love with everyone and everything. Human love usually manifests itself in kindness, respect, and service.

You and I and *everyone without exception* are loved *at every moment of our lives unconditionally* by God. Not even one's rejection of God or our sinfulness removes us from that love. When we say "God is mercy," we stress the undeserved and caring nature of God's love for us, so let us not deny the reality of God's love for us because of a sense of unworthiness, our temperament, our doubts, or our sometimes embrace of evil and its many attractive taunts. *All creation*, including you and me, always *flows from God, yet remains in God.* The New Testament's Acts of the Apostles (17–28) puts so beautifully yet literally: God "in whom we live, and move, and have our being." This is the content of our faith and the meaning and source of our lives—not simply *keeping the rules* and going to worship. God is not our judge but rather our *safety net.*

Since we believe that the Son Jesus from the beginning was to become one of us and in his humanity part of creation, there had to be the possibility of a human body/spirit *suitable* to receive the incarnation of the second person of the Trinity. We know historically that became possible only within the recent 10,000 years of human development when *Homo sapiens* became capable of exercising not only free will but also advanced rationality. How incredibly fortunate we are to be alive after this possibility became real over two thousand years ago in Jesus Christ. Through Christ living with us as one of us, we have come to know that God not only loves us but God also *likes* us: "Playing in the world: And my delights were to be with the children of men" (Prov. 8:31).

Not only by faith are we drawn to the life and mystery of the Risen Christ, we know through the living Church that we ourselves are missioned to be *co-creators of a redeemed but unfinished world* (reaffirmed by a major teaching of the Second Vatican Council.) Through the gift of Jesus and God's love we recognize our union with God, and that a true response must be a life centered in bringing that deep and creative love to an unfinished world. God also takes care of us when we die; before that, we are all responsible for one another. What we rightly perceive as *evils* in life are really *gaps* or *holes* which must be filled by people and structures which fill them with the products of love: injustice with justice, poverty with sharing, discord with forgiveness, infidelity with fidelity, rejection with acceptance, lies with truth, ignorance with knowledge, separation with inclusion, war with peace, etc.

COMPLETING THE WORLD WITH GOD

He told them another parable:
"The kingdom of heaven is like a mustard seed,
which a man took and planted in his field.
Though it is the smallest of all seeds, yet when it grows,
it is the largest of garden plants and becomes a tree,
so that the birds come and perch in its branches."
(Mt. 13:31–32)

"First there was God—only God. There has always been God. Then there was the first atom of matter—the first thing other than God."

The tiny, tiny atom—yet it was the beginning of creation. *"Though it is the smallest of all seeds...it becomes a tree."*

Our countless human co-creative acts add new leaves, branches, strength, and life to what God began with the tree of creation. This is the *story* which I propose to guide us with enthusiasm and hope through our life's mission and purpose.

Were the first fourteen billion years of creation wasted? No, because it was God's plan that was always developing step-by-step, until humanity became modern *Homo sapiens* and could manifest itself as created in the *image and likeness of God* (possessing a more developed *reason* and *free will* and inhabiting a hospitable Earth). This set the stage for humanity to participate as *co-creators of a redeemed but unfinished world.*

As our story continues, we must remember that *every person at her or his core—where God is ever-present—is good and loved by God.* When we see the horrors of history—even the daily news—it can be easy to forget this. God's loving plan for creation knew about (not caused) all this *in advance*. How this will be integrated and healed we know not, but God knows—and our faith-filled response is: *trust*. Creation and life were never meant to make sense without God.

When we speak of humans' first attempts to respond to God's plan that we should become *co-creators* with God of an unfinished world, our story can move quickly past inventing the wheel, the taming of fire, the development of language and art, and the growing *control* of primitive technologies. Throughout our history, almost incredible challenges have been successfully met and integrated—and give promise that the *holes* which are still masking real evils can be filled by the effects of loving human response.

The scriptural paradigm—the *only* place where Jesus himself gives *the* criterion for human salvation (i.e., the fulfillment of our life's meaning)—is in the Gospel of Matthew, "I was hungry and you gave me food, I was thirsty and you gave me drink, a stranger and you welcomed me, naked and you clothed me, ill and you cared for me, in prison and you visited me... When did we see you? Whatever you did for one of these least brothers of mine, you did for me" (Mt. 25:34–46). Think of the countless concrete instances of caring human interventions in the whole world every day which directly address Jesus's challenges in Matthew. They are frequent and overwhelming. Add to that the remarkable *new* advances in medicine, technology, social interaction, education, cultural interaction, lessening world poverty, etc. We can become so accustomed to positive growth that the excitement and joy of co-creation is diminished. And we must speak of that most common and profound example of human love and service which is the *family!* In spite of the many challenges involved, self-giving, sacrifice, work, generosity, service, and love each day are recommitted to and embraced in hundreds of ways—and *most* people are true to their commitments and hopes.

Our wise and holy friend, Pope Francis, strongly advises us, "Just as you cannot understand Christ apart from the kingdom he came to bring, so, too, your personal mission is inseparable from the building of that kingdom... Your identification with Christ and his will involves a commitment to build with him that kingdom of love, justice, and universal peace. Christ himself wants to experience this with you, in all the efforts and sacrifices that it entails, but also in all the joy and enrichment it brings. You cannot grow in holiness without committing yourself, body and soul, to giving your best to this endeavor." (*Gaudete et Exultate*, March 19, 2018)

Co-create with God.

OVERCOMING THE OBSTACLES

May I suggest two major obstacles: one is truly *our fault* and the other is more subtle and gradual, but if unknowingly embraced could sadly lead to a life of mediocrity. Our every word so far has laid out God's perpetual love, respect, and closeness to each of us. Even sin would not cancel God's love for us, but some people might think it has. And most people don't really know what sin is. True sin is *our fault,* whether it is something we do or some good we know we should do but will not. It is a decision and is destructive. It tears at the beautiful fabric of our lives. Instead of filling *holes*, it creates new ones. Temptation puts us up on the *high wire*. Our only *balancing pole* has character on one end and conscience on the other—as we *bargain* to *have our cake and eat it, too*. Sometimes we safely walk to the other side out of temptation; sometimes we fall. Sins are *little deaths*, but Christ always has power over death and is eager to heal us if and when we *wake up* again to his constant friendship. We observed earlier that God was not a *judge* (our *truth* is our judge), but acts always as our *safety net* under the high wire.

Most good *practicing Catholics* grew up thinking simply that sin was *not keeping the rules*. Admit it. And if I broke a big rule and couldn't/wouldn't change, I thought it was *all over*. If I disagreed with a Church rule (or teaching), then I thought I was, again, *not a good Catholic.* These were conclusions in a *juridic* Church (i.e., *keep the laws and rules!*)—adequate for immature children; devastatingly contradictory to the freeing Gospel of Jesus Christ. And if I saw myself as *not a good Catholic,* then why go through the motions as I drift away from Mass, sacraments, and the support of a faith-community (and the wonderful realities of which we have just read)? That would most likely lead to a life of mediocrity. Do not settle for it.

As urgent and enjoyable as it might be, this is not the place (nor space!) for showing how all the statements above are true to the Catholic Church, to history, to human reasoning—and to God's self-revelation. Read, think, pray, and ponder—rejoicing in God's unconditional love for you which will never end. Accept God's invitation to live consciously each day as a co-creator of an unfinished world. Every saint was also a sinner—as are you and I—but we're working on it.

ABOUT THE AUTHOR

Msgr. Dennis Regan is a Roman Catholic priest of the Diocese of Rockville Centre, New York, and has a doctorate in sacred theology. He has served as rector and professor of Moral Theology at Immaculate Conception Seminary at Huntington, New York, and adjunct professor at Fordham University and St. John's University. For Catholic Health Services of Long Island, he was senior vice president for Mission and Bioethics.

He has pastored two large parishes on Long Island, and presented Study Weeks for army chaplains, clergy, and laity on topics of medical ethics, sexuality and marriage, and social justice throughout the United States.

He was honored to serve on the board of directors of Covenant House (international).

Extensive foreign travel helped him appreciate the wonderful cultures and people in God's world, with racquetball and white-water rafting helping him keep his sanity.